"Bobby has written *Tactics* to awaker
has a plan to place an eternal crown
a life that honors Him and His will.
the enemy has a plan to get us to quit and give up
finished. *Tactics* will encourage you, increase your faith, and awaken you
to the tactics of the enemy."

Rev. Dr. Samuel Rodriguez, Lead Pastor
New Season Christian Worship Center and President of the
National Hispanic Christian Leadership Conference (NHCLC)

"We live in a time when the enemy is desperately seeking to destroy God's
plan for His people. The best way to thwart the enemy's advancements
is to know how they intend to destroy you. Bobby Gourley has written
a timely book that shines a light onto Satan's tactics in such a way as
to destroy any chance of his success. I would highly recommend this
book to anyone serious about walking according to God's plan while
disrupting the distractions of the enemy."

Pastor Jim Kubic, Launchpoint Church, Lebanon, TN

"This is not only Bobby's first book but I can tell you that it is one of the
most practical and helpful books I have ever read. This is perfect both for
the new Christian but also for the person who has never come to Christ
in faith. It is even an evangelistic tool to give to your unsaved friends. It
is practical, pastoral, biblical, simple and theologically sound. You will
be amazed at the insights in this book. They come page after page."

Dr. R.T. Kendall, Senior Pastor, Westminster Chapel
London, England and author of *Total Forgiveness*,
The Anointing: Yesterday, Today, and Tomorrow & *Holy Fire*

"I want to commend Pastor Bobby Gourley's book *Tactics* to you.
Bobby's insight theologically is current yet rooted in the principles of
Scripture which are not limited by time. He has in this book taken a
trip through Scripture and made it applicable to today's challenges to
give opportunity for victory. His insights will create a discernment
and understanding through the Holy Spirit to expose the tactics of the

enemy who tried to destroy your destiny. Theologically sound teaching validated by authenticity in lifestyle is hard to find in today culture, but Bobby Gourley has found that balance and I commend his book and teaching to you."

Pastor Dave Deerman, Lead Pastor
CenterPointe Church, Bowling Green, KY

Bobby Gourley speaks with such wisdom and conviction about the tactics of the enemy, but more importantly the plan of God! You can instantly tell that his strength about this topic comes from personal experience and what he has personally survived. This is a must read, do yourself a favor, learn from a season Bobby survived and get this book!

Pastor Adrian Davis, Senior Pastor
All Nations Worship Assembly, Huntsville, AL
Author, Leader, and Designer

We live in world that is dazed and confused, in search of a sense of meaning and a place of belonging. My friend Bobby Gurley's new book, Tactics, will help you and anyone who reads it-connect with the God who designed and crafted you to walk out a life of purpose that extends in its significance from here into eternity. Read it and let it light a fire of hope on the inside of you!

Lee Cummings, Senior Leader of Radiant Church and
Radiant Network of Churches based in Kalamazoo Michigan

Author of "Flourish-Planting Your LifeWhere God Designed It to Thrive"

Whether you have been a believer for three days or 30 years, this book is vital to understanding your purpose on this Earth. Pastor Bobby Gourley does an exceptional job showcasing God's plan for your life in this book!

Pastor Tyler Sterban, Student Pastor
Potential Church, Cooper City, FL

BOBBY GOURLEY

TACTICS

God's Plan
for Your Life
and the Enemy's
Plan to Stop It

ISBN 978-0-578-45707-9

First paperback edition April 2019

Cover design and interior design by Dede Simmons

www.bobbygourley.com

Acknowledgments

Writing a book has been more difficult than I thought and more rewarding than I could have ever dreamed. None of this would have been possible without my wife, Toyia. You have seen the best in me when no one else could, and you have encouraged and prayed what you saw to life in me.

To my children. Thank you for your encouragement, your sacrifice and your motivation. Each one of you, Alicia, Ariah, Ariana, and R.J., have taught me more about life, God and myself than any book or person.

I'm eternally grateful to the elders and staff at Chapel that believe in me, pray for me, and encourage me to step out in faith to pursue everything God has in His plans for us at Chapel. Thank you for believing in me and with me, and walking beside me.

Through the writing process, I have learned that writing is not a solo endeavor, but a team journey. God blessed me with some amazing teammates. Thank you, Margaret for your constant encouragement, accountability and motivation; without which, this book would still be in my head and not on paper. Thank you, Sara for using your incredible gift to help bring my dream and words to life. You are a master of words and encouragement. Thank you, Dede for sacrificing your time and energy to present this message in a beautiful way. Thank you, Shirley Moseley and Carlene Blackburn for you for your attention to detail to ensure the final book would be reflected through excellence. Thank you, Dr. Kendall for awakening me to my gift and for encouraging me to walk in it. Thank you, Jennifer for believing in me and this book and helping get it to the world. To everyone else that has had a part in this journey thank you! It is because of your efforts and encouragement that I have a legacy to pass on to my family where one didn't exist before.

Finally, to Jesus, my Savior, my Lord, my Help, and my Rock, I thank you for your voice, your Word, and your mercy. I have learned through the ups and the downs that you are constantly with me and fighting for me to fulfill your plan. Your love and salvation are my greatest blessings and motivation.

Foreword

For several years I preached regularly at Christ Chapel in Florence, Alabama. This was when their pastor, E.M. "Doc" Shell, an old and beloved friend, invited me there. I was there at Word Spirit Power conferences with Jack Taylor and Charles Carrin. I was there with the late John Paul Jackson. I went there by myself as well. A while after Doc Shell retired, he asked me, "Do you know anyone who might succeed me at Christ Chapel?"

My answer: Yes, Bobby Gourley from nearby Nashville, Tennessee. But who is Bobby Gourley? No one in Florence had ever heard of him. I urged them to invite him to preach so they could decide for themselves. They did, and they called him. Although following Doc Shell was no small challenge, he and his wife Toyia have not only won the hearts of the people at Christ Chapel but it has seen remarkable growth as well. He has done this because he is what I call a Word and Spirit man. He believes the Word and the Spirit must not be separated but joined together. It is his consistent expository preaching of the
Word and openness to the Holy Spirit that explains Bobby Gourley's success in a relatively short period of time.

As I urged the church in Florence, Alabama to listen to him, I urge you to read this book. It is common to look for a well-known author when you shop for a book. In much the same way my wife Louise and I find out who the actors are before we see a film. The problem with this however is that we tend to miss a lot of good films!

This is not only Bobby's first book but I can tell you that it is one of the most practical and helpful books I have ever read. This is perfect both for the new Christian but also for the person who has never come to Christ in faith. It is even an evangelistic tool to give to your unsaved friends.

It is practical, pastoral, biblical, simple and theologically sound. You will be amazed at the insights in this book. They come page after page. Buy copies for your friends and they will thank you – just as the people of Christ Chapel thank me for recommending Bobby Gourley to them.

– R. T. KENDALL, MINISTER
WESTMINSTER CHAPEL
LONDON (1977-2002)

Contents

1

Crowns

Do you not know that in a race all the runners run, but only one gets the prize? Run in such a way as to get the prize.
1 Corinthians 9:24 (NIV)

Jill sat in an auditorium surrounded by friends and family, her palms sweating with anticipation. Although she tried to sit still, her nervous energy was causing her to fidget. The man at the front of the room was sharing stories about the people seated around her. He would call out a name, and then state how proud he was of that person's hard work, perseverance and character. The memories he shared of each person revealed his deep fatherly pride. As he concluded each story, the audience members would celebrate that person with vigorous clapping, whistling, and shouts of excitement. It was a powerful atmosphere of celebration and encouragement.

Jill was so caught up in celebrating her friends as their names were called, she didn't hear her own name being called. The girl seated next to her nudged her. "Jill, he's calling for you," she said. Startled, Jill got to her feet and made her way to the stage, taking her place next to the man.

Being the center of attention made Jill nervous, so she fixed her eyes on the table beside the man where she saw her name in large gold letters: Jill Jones. She heard the man share how proud he was of her; how much she had grown since he first met her; how hard she had worked to improve in everything he had taught her. He mentioned the times she had overcome obstacles, made mistakes and even fallen flat on her face, yet each time she'd gotten back up to try again. He spoke of her great character and the sacrificial love she had shown friends and family, and said how proud of her he was and grateful for all her efforts.

He turned to Jill. "When I first met you" he said, "I saw your potential. I knew what you were capable of if you would trust me to help you. I made it my goal to help you see what I saw, and I was with you every step of the way. I know it wasn't easy. I watched you try, make mistakes, become frustrated. I was there when you fell and injured your ankle. The intense pain made you cry. Remember what I told you? 'Pain is temporary but glory is forever'. I remember carrying you to get help, yet how determined you were to return and cheer on your friends. You gave them the encouragement they needed and even put yourself back out there, regardless of the pain." She looked up and he smiled at her. "Jill, your pain was temporary, but now your glory is forever," he declared.

Tears of joy rolled down Jill's cheeks. Friends and family clapped and cheered as the man reached for the item she had been focusing on. He held it up where everyone could see her name shining in the light, then placed it in her hands. Jill hugged it to her chest as she walked back to her seat. Her family and friends were still clapping and cheering as she sat down.

Mesmerized, she drank in every detail of her treasure, the beautiful wooden base stained a rich dark brown, its sleek edges expertly crafted. Her full name was engraved upon a gleaming gold medal. Her fingers moved slowly over the letters J I L L J O N E S. She gazed at the real focal point of the item, a golden figure of a girl kicking a soccer ball. This was not just any trophy. This was her reward for finishing the season. This was recognition from her coach that she was part of his team, the championship team!

After the ceremony Jill and her friends gathered to compare trophies while their moms and dads took countless photos. Later, Jill's mom and dad flooded Facebook and Instagram with photos of their little girl holding up her first trophy.

At home, Jill asked her parents if she could place her trophy on the fireplace mantle where everyone could see it. Of course they said yes. Each time Jill went into the living room, she would look at the golden letters of her name and recall her coach's speech and the championship season. Visitors were often exhorted to the story of Jill's soccer trophy by Jill herself!

Do you remember receiving your first trophy? What was it for? Little league baseball? Soccer? A piano recital? Band? An art project? How did you feel when you received it? Excited? Proud? Joyous?

For most of us, it has been a long time since we received a trophy. Adults rarely get trophies at work. Instead, our employers tend to give us paychecks, thank God! However, did you know that you are still in a race to receive a trophy, and that it is the most important trophy you will ever receive — one with eternal rewards and glory? This trophy truly demonstrates that pain is temporary and glory is forever. In fact it will never rust nor will it fade. This trophy will last forever.

> *"Blessed is the man who remains steadfast under trial, for when he has stood the test he will receive the crown of life, which God has promised to those who love Him."*
> **James 1:12 (ESV)**

God's Desire

God wants to give you a crown of life for overcoming the hardships in this life. He is your Coach who is trying to help you fulfill the potential He placed deep inside of you when He created you. He wants to see your redemptive potential realized. He wants you to trust Him even when He has to discipline you. He wants to pick you up when you fall and empower you to move forward. He wants to see you grow and persevere through difficult seasons, and become the champion He created you to be. Just as Jill's coach publicly honored her, God wants to stand in front of your friends and family and express His pride and love for you as He presents you with a crown of life.

God's desire is to present you with an eternal trophy at the end of your life. He wants to see you finish life's race as a champion. It won't happen by accident. He has a plan to see you receive your trophy and He is always working His plan. In fact, His plan is unfolding right before your very eyes, and it will come to pass. To determine whether or not you receive God's trophy depends on one thing: will you submit your life to God's Son, Jesus, and His plan for your life, or will you submit to the enemy's plan for your life, which disqualifies you from receiving a crown of life?

As Bob Dylan sang in his Grammy-winning hit, *Gotta Serve Somebody*:

> *You may be an ambassador to England or France*
> *You may like to gamble, you might like to dance*
> *You may be the heavyweight champion of the world*
> *You may be a socialite with a long string of pearls*
>
> *Chorus*
> *But you're going to have to serve somebody, yes indeed*
> *You're going to have to serve somebody*
> *Well, it may be the devil or it may be the Lord*
> *But you're going to have to serve somebody*

Believe me when I say this, God has a plan for your life, but so does the enemy. Regardless of what the world or popular culture tell you, you must choose whose plan you will follow: God's or the enemy's.

> "Blessed is the man who remains steadfast under trial, for when he has stood the test he will receive the crown of life, which God has promised to those who love him. Let no one say when he is tempted, I am being tempted by God, for God cannot be tempted with evil, and he himself tempts no one. But each person is tempted when he is lured and enticed by his own desire. Then desire when it has conceived gives birth to sin, and sin when it is fully grown brings forth death. Do not be deceived, my beloved brothers." **James 1:12-16 (ESV)**

In the previous verse, James reveals God's plan, as well as the enemy's tactics to disrupt God's plan for your life. In his best-selling book, "Victory in Spiritual Warfare," Dr. Tony Evans teaches in depth on James 1:12-16[1]. I highly recommend you read his book (after this one, of course). However, for our purpose, I have summarized a few key points:

God has a plan for eternal DESTINY for your life.

The enemy has a plan to tempt you away from your destiny with your own DESIRES.

The enemy will use DECEPTION to get you to think that your desires are God's desires.

The enemy will turn your deception into DISOBEDIENCE.

Then enemy will let your disobedience grow into DEATH.

God has a plan to turn your death into DESTINY.

Tactics: an action or strategy carefully planned to achieve a specific end.

Knowledge is power. When you know God's plan and the enemy's tactics, you will have a much better chance of standing in front of God as He places a crown of life upon your head. My prayer throughout this book is that you can live a victorious and impactful life that overcomes every temptation the enemy plans against you by giving you the knowledge and the truth of his tactics. As they used to say at the end of every G.I. Joe episode I watched growing up, "Now I know, and knowing is half the battle." Once you know the enemy's plan, you must work to stop it from disrupting God's plan for your life.

2

Plans

"For I know the plans I have for you," declares the LORD, "plans to prosper you and not to harm you, plans to give you hope and a future."
Jeremiah 29:11 (NIV)

I have incredible news for you, news that has the power to bring hope to your soul and excitement to your life. Yes, this news is able to alter both your current perspective and future outlook. Here is the news: God, who created everything, including you and me, has a plan for your life. You were not created by accident, nor does your life happen by chance. You are part of a grand cosmic plan.

God is an inventive and creative God. Unfortunately, I believe we often take a narrow view of His creative power. We tend to focus on His artistry and visual expressions of creativity, and although God is indeed creative and expressive, He is also inventive. According to the Oxford English Dictionary, the word invent means "to create or design (something that has not existed before); be the originator of." The primary difference between a creator and an inventor is that a creator tends to create as a form of expression, while an inventor typically creates something to fulfill a purpose. Creativity is intimate, expressive and artistic. It involves the heart. Inventing is skillful, knowledgeable and forward-thinking. It involves the mind. God is both creator and inventor.

Every inventor begins the creative process with a purpose and end result in mind. An inventor develops creations to fulfill a purpose or solve a problem. For example, Thomas Edison sought to rid the world of darkness by inventing the light bulb. Elon Musk wanted to invent a car that worked for his family and protected the environment by reducing the need for fossil fuels. Dr. Patricia Bath wanted to prevent blindness and make cataract surgery safer and more economical, so she invented the laser probe that revolutionized the precision, results and cost of cataract surgery.

God invented you. When He invented you, He was thinking ahead. He had in mind the purpose you would fulfill, the issues you would resolve, and ultimately the meaning of your existence. You are no accident, and neither is your life.

God created you

When God created you, He exercised all of His powerful creativity. Just look at you! There is no one like you. Even if you have an identical twin, you still do not act, think or dream identically. American pastor and author, Mark Batterson says, "There has never been anyone like you. That is not a testament to you, but to the God who created you!"

Creation is an intimate process. All artists, whether sculptors, musicians, dancers, filmmakers or some other creative pursuit, are intimately connected to their work. Their life is enmeshed in their work because it is an extension of their heart, mind and soul. For creatives, their creations are an expression of their inner-most thoughts, emotions and passions.

God is a creative God. He created you and me. This means God is intimate with His creation. In the creation account of Genesis, we see God's creative power and intimacy displayed. In Genesis 1 it says that God created the heavens and the earth. How did He create the heavens and the earth? He spoke them into existence. That is some power. It also says that He created all of our environment, including all animals, fish, and nature. How did He create all of our environment and living things?

You guessed it. He spoke them into existence. He was showing off His creative power. The Genesis account then says that He created man and woman. How did He create man and woman? No, He didn't speak them into existence. He changed His technique.

Imagine God creating the entire universe. He said, "Let there be galaxies," and BOOM! galaxies exploded onto the scene. He said, "Let there be water," and BOOM! oceans, seas, and rivers began to flow. He said, "Let there be chickens," and BOOM! Chick-fil-A's popped up all over the place. God is on a roll, speaking everything into existence. At the sound of His voice something new comes on the scene. Once He says, "Let there be..." BOOM!, it is. He does this over and over again. Then, all of a sudden He slows down. He transitions from the powerful display of creativity in LET THERE BE to the intimate display of creativity in LET US MAKE. Genesis describes God's technique as forming us. He wanted to use His hands, not just His voice. He reached down and began to form us with His very own hands.

Now, close your eyes and place yourself in the story. God is creating the universe by speaking with power and authority. Suddenly, He slows down and says, "Let us make (insert your name)." He begins forming you out of dirt with His very own hands, like He's molding clay or playing with Play-doh (disregard the smell). As you watch Him develop your body, you hear Him describe what you will look like, what kind of personality you will have, and the dreams He is placing in your heart. He is describing your purpose. God created you with His very own hands. You are not an accident. You were not formed as a mass production of an intergalactic assembly line. You are custom-made by the great inventor and creator, God! His fingerprints are all over you! Even more astounding, your image reflects the very image of God!

Do you grasp the gravity of the truth that God is not just a creator or inventor, but YOUR Creator and Inventor? Knowing this, you should also realize that He has a plan and purpose for your life. He has a personal investment in you. God knows you better than anyone else. He created every cell in your body. King David of Israel discovered this truth and it helped him become a man after God's own heart. David wrote in Psalm 139:

'For you created my inmost being;
You knit me together in my mother's womb.
 I praise You because I am fearfully and wonderfully made;
Your works are wonderful,
I know that full well.
 My frame was not hidden from You
when I was made in the secret place,
when I was woven together in the depths of the earth.
 Your eyes saw my unformed body;
all the days ordained for me were written in
Your book before one of them came to be.'

Psalm 139:13-16 (NIV)

God knows you better than anyone else, and loves you more than anyone else! He has a personal stake in your life, and wants to see your full heavenly potential realized. He created you on purpose and with a purpose. First and foremost, He wants you to be saved and spend eternity with Him. God desires EVERY person to be saved. He says so in 1 Timothy 2:3-4 and John 3:16.

"This is good, and pleases God our Savior, who wants all people to be saved and to come to a knowledge of the truth." **1 Timothy 2:3-4 (NIV)**

"For God so loved the world that he gave his one and only Son, that whoever believes in him shall not perish but have eternal life." **John 3:16 (NIV)**

The Westminster Catechism

What is your purpose? What is our purpose? God's people and the church have routinely asked the same question. The Westminster Catechism is one of the ways the church has attempted to answer these questions. It is a confession of the Christian faith, drafted in the 1600s by 151 theologians at Westminster Abbey. It is a series of questions followed by Bible-based answers that serves as a doctrinal standard for many Christian churches throughout the world today. The first question of the Westminster Catechism (Christian confession of faith) asks, "What is the purpose of man?" The answer is, "To know God and enjoy Him forever." God wants you to reach your redemptive potential. In other words, He wants you to grow spiritually into the image of Jesus. In Romans, Paul explains it this way: "For those whom he foreknew he also predestined to be conformed to the image of his Son, in order that he might be the firstborn among many brothers." **Romans 8:29 (ESV)**

God wants you to live and love like Jesus, act and react like Jesus, and reflect His image as you live your life. The Bible says this is God's will for your life. Another scripture puts it this way: "For this is the will of God, your sanctification: that you abstain from sexual immorality." **1 Thessalonians 4:3 (ESV)**

Understanding Sanctification

Sanctification is a big word that means you allow what God has done on the inside of you to affect every area of your life, including your sex life. Yes, your sexuality and God's will are intertwined, so if you have ever wondered if God is concerned with your sex life, He is. God does not compartmentalize your life. He wants all of it! Jesus affirms this truth in **Mark 12:29-30 (ESV)**. In this passage, Jesus was asked by one of the scribes what the most important commandment of all was, and He responded, *"The most important is, 'Hear, O Israel: The Lord our God, the Lord is one. And you shall love the Lord your God with all your heart and with all your soul and with all your mind and with all your strength.'* God wants all of your heart, mind, soul and body. He wants your life and sexuality to align with His will for you. Your sexuality and sex life are God's business and abstaining from sexual immorality is an essential part of the sanctification process.

In addition to saying no to sexual immorality, the process of sanctification means you become more and more dependent upon God and less dependent upon yourself. You become more sensitive to sin and more in awe of grace. You grow more aware of the Holy Spirit and His voice, His leading, and His desires. The Bible describes this as working out your salvation.

> "Therefore, my beloved, as you have always obeyed, so now, not only as in my presence but much more in my absence, work out your own salvation with fear and trembling, for it is God who works in you, both to will and to work for his good pleasure." **Philippians 2:12-13 (ESV)**

God wants to see what He has done on the inside of us radiate to the outside, and impact our minds, behavior, actions, speech, attitudes, and relationships. He wants the world to see what He already sees inside us, and it is our job to work it out.

Sanctification is like learning about your salvation in reverse. Let me explain. I have four amazing, beautiful, intelligent children that are better than all other children in every conceivable way! Okay, so I'm biased. Anyway, I have four children that I love. I was there when each one was born. And when they were born, I loved them more than they could ever imagine. I knew instinctively that I would do anything and everything to protect them, provide for them, and show them that I love them. I also knew that I would sacrifice whatever was necessary to take care of them. Why? Because they are my kids, my son and my daughters. The moment they were born, they were 100 percent my children. They will never be more or less my kids. My love will not increase or decrease after they are born (although there are some days when this is tested!). In short, I know how much I love them and all that I will do to provide and protect them. The problem is that my kids have no idea what it means to be my son or daughter. They don't know what I will do to protect them or how I will provide for them. They will spend the rest of their lives learning what it means to be my children. They will learn to trust and obey me and whatever else I teach them. They will also learn all the privileges of being a son or daughter of mine.

Much in the same way, when you are saved, you are completely God's son or daughter. His love doesn't increase or decrease. He knows everything you have access to in His Kingdom, and how far He will go to provide for and protect you. The problem is when you get saved you have no idea what it means to be a son or daughter of God! You will spend the rest of your life learning what it means to be His child and what happened to you in the incredible moment when you said yes to His son and His grace, and He saved you! To simplify, you receive everything God has for you at salvation, but it takes your entire life, and then some, to learn what you received. Sanctification is learning what God has done on the inside of you when He saved you, and allowing it to permeate your spirit, mind, body, speech, relationships, decisions and lifestyle.

To recap what we've learned, so far: God has a plan. He is working out His plan. You are part of His plan. It is a good plan. It is an eternal plan. Jesus said that He came that you may have life and have it more abundantly (John 10:10). This is the good news.

So what are God's plans for your life? I'm glad you asked. Generally, His plan is for you to know Him intimately, enjoy Him eternally, and advance His purposes here on earth. To summarize, He wants you to fulfill

His Great Commission by applying the Great Commandment. I'm sure by now you're thinking, "Wow! That's great theology, but what about His plans for me specifically?" Your specific purpose is to fulfill the Great Commission through your uniquely created personality, gifting and talents within the context of your relationships and life. This means that God wants you to advance His purposes right where He has placed you at this specific time. Don't wait until you move, or are in ministry, or get older. Let God use you right now.

The Enemy Has a Plan for Your Life

Now that I've shared the good news, I unfortunately have to share some bad news. Just as God has a plan for your life, so does the Enemy; only his plan is to disrupt, stop and discourage you from being a part of God's plan.

The enemy has a plan in place to disrupt every promise, blessing and purpose for your life. It is nothing personal. He doesn't get emotionally attached to his mission. He doesn't think you are special. He just has an agenda against God and everyone God loves. He knows that God's greatest desire is to redeem people, and to pour His love and blessings into and through them. Therefore, he wants to cause as much disruption to God's plan as possible. He began by challenging Adam and Eve's faith in God's word and promises given to mankind in the Garden of Eden, and he has continued in this same tactic with every single promise given from God to people since. As soon as God gives a promise, the enemy swoops in to bring confusion, doubt and obstacles to the promise. For example:

- God promised Abraham that he would be the father of many nations. The enemy used delay and doubt to tempt Abraham to try to fulfill God's promise on his own.

- God promised Joseph that he would rule over his brothers.
  The enemy used jealousy and hate to cause Joseph's brothers
  to plot his death and sell him into slavery.

- God anointed David king over all Israel. The enemy used Saul's
  jealousy to try to kill David and run him out of Israel.

- God promised Israel a messiah, born of a virgin, who would
  save the world. The enemy used fear and lust for power
  to get Herod to kill all newborns in hopes of killing the messiah.

The Thief

In John 10:10, Jesus states, *"The thief comes only to steal and kill and destroy. I came that they may have life and have it abundantly."* As we learned in the previous chapter, God is a life-giving God. He is constantly pursuing what is best for us. However, in the first part of this verse, we see the enemy's purpose and passion. This scripture clearly illustrates the cosmic battle over you and me. The enemy is trying to bring pain, suffering, and death into the world, but Jesus brings abundant, everlasting, joyful and fulfilling life into the world — and we are the battleground!

In Mark 3:23, Jesus is teaching people about the tactics of the enemy when he shares an illustration about a strong man. *"How can anyone break into the house of a strong man and steal his things, unless he first ties up the strong man? Then he can take everything."* (CEV) In this parable, Satan is the strong man, but Jesus is stronger. He is the one who overpowers Satan and strips him of his armor.

Satan is a defeated foe. He knows. Jesus knows. But many times we live as if we don't know this truth. Satan is powerless over us. He cannot remove us from God's grip. He cannot destroy our soul. He cannot control us. All he can do is tempt us to give up our promises. The enemy

25

wants to steal what God has given us. Why? He doesn't have anything of his own. He cannot take anything that was not his to begin with. He has no rights to it. What does he want to steal?

The enemy wants to steal your **worship**. (Job 1)

The enemy wants to steal your **faith**. (Luke 22:31-32)
The enemy wants to steal your **joy**. (Nehemiah 8:10)

The enemy wants to steal your **hope**. He wants you to live in a failed past instead of looking forward to your glorious future.

The enemy wants to steal your **peace**. He wants you to wait for heaven to experience the peace you could have right here and right now.

The enemy wants to steal your **godly reputation**. He wants to discredit you.

The enemy wants to steal your **promise** just like he did Adam and Eve's.

Beware of Him Who Has Nothing to Lose

The enemy fights to the death. He has nothing to lose. When I was a teenager I thought I was tough. I listened to rap, and aspired to the gangsta lifestyle. Sure, a lot of teenagers go through an identity crisis, but I let mine go too far. I hung out with people who acted like thugs, and I got involved in things I should not have. I remember my dad telling me to beware of people who have nothing to lose. He said that since they have nothing to lose, they fear no consequences to their actions and will go to greater extremes than anyone can handle. He taught me that a person with nothing to lose will be more violent than someone who has a lot to lose. In looking back over my life experiences, I have seen my dad's words of wisdom proven true time and time again.

Satan has absolutely nothing to lose. He will stop at nothing to disrupt God's plan for your life, even if it means killing. He will kill your dreams. He will kill your body. His ultimate plan is to destroy everything God has created. He wanted to see heaven destroyed, so he mounted an anarchy and failed. He wanted to see God's creation destroyed, so he convinced Adam and Eve that God was against them instead of for them. He wants to destroy you and God's purpose for your life.

The Greek word for destroy in John 10:10 is apollymi. According to Strong's Concordance, it means to destroy; to put out of the way entirely; abolish; put an end to; ruin; render useless; to kill; to declare that one must be put to death; to devote or give over to eternal misery in hell; to perish; and to be lost[3]. Whoa! This is not a tactic for the faint of heart. The enemy is trying to get you out of the way. He wants to give you over to hell. He wants to render you useless. And, if you are going to go to heaven, he wants to make you useless on earth.

The enemy's plan is to prevent you from experiencing God's eternal life. If he can't stop you from experiencing eternal life, he will seek to steal any of the blessings God has promised for you during your earthly life. **If he can't stop you from getting to heaven, he will try to render you and your life useless on earth.** This is his desire and his purpose, but how does he do it?

3

Blame

Why do you see the speck that is in your brother's eye,
but do not notice the log that is in your own eye?
Matthew 7:3 (ESV)

Life is not an easy journey. No one ever said it would be. It is filled with peaks and valleys, twists and turns, and unforeseen obstacles. Each day we face spiritual battles. Some are minor and some are major. We know this. It is our experience, and we have the scars to prove it. For some, the battle comes in the form of physical pain, sickness, injury or disease. For others, it presents itself as emotional pain, abuse, heartbreak, depression, anxiety or conflict. Still for others, it is the struggle to overcome fears, failure and financial issues.

> *"Therefore do not worry about tomorrow,*
> *for tomorrow will worry about itself.*
> *Each day has enough trouble of its own."*
> **~Jesus, Sermon on the Mount, Matthew 6:34 (ESV)**

Every year, our church leaves the comforts of America, Starbucks and Chick-fil-A to go to Haiti and serve the incredible people there. Once we are off the plane and making our way through the city, I always note the looks of shock on our team member's faces as they take in the extreme poverty of Haiti, from the trash piles on its beautiful beaches, to weary people calling desperately for help. The reality of people living in poverty day in and day out creates a stark contrast with the tremendously blessed lives we experience here in the USA.

While in Haiti, we work with a local Christian orphanage. Our team loves playing with the children; many of whom are the same age as our team members. It's a joy to witness how young people with so many differences can connect so easily simply by sharing universally fun activities like doing each others hair, playing soccer and even rough-housing.

On our last trip, there was a young boy named Junior that our team fell in love with due to his warm and magnetic personality. Everyone kept talking about how much they loved Junior. One night, after a long day of ministry, we had our daily devotional, worship and debrief time. It was during this time that all of our team began talking about how much fun they had with Junior. Then, my wife, who leads the trips, shared Junior's story. She told them that he lives in the orphanage because both of his parents died of HIV, which Junior contracted through the womb. Since he was HIV positive, no one wanted him or his disease. Our team was speechless at the notion that a boy full of so much life and love had been abandoned through disease, hopelessness and poverty. You could see the tears well up in their eyes as they took in the gravity of Junior's story. Why does one child seem to have the world handed to him in America, while another child elsewhere seems to have his world torn apart. Although I could dive into a great theological and philosophical discussion, the simple truth of the matter is life is not fair, and many times our life experiences are outside of our control.

The Victim Mentality

Oftentimes, when life does not go the way we expect or want, we look for someone to blame. When things go sideways, there is always a very real temptation to view ourselves as a victim. Giving into this temptation leads to a "victim mentality," a condition in which the mind is able to immediately produce a thousand reasons that excuse our failures and validate our innocence in every unfortunate situation we encounter. Looking for someone to blame enables us to shift responsibility for negative outcomes away from ourselves and appoint it to another person. Unfortunately, when we point fingers at others as the cause of all our heartaches, failures and pain, instead of taking ownership of our lives, we set in motion a continuous cycle of failure and bad decisions.

Recently, I was invited to attend a drug court graduation. If you are unfamiliar with drug court, it is a strategy many court systems have adopted in order to help drug addicts overcome their addiction and clear their record of drug charges. Offenders must complete a court-appointed process of restoration that includes attending meetings, doing community service, taking random drug screenings, and fulfilling all other court-appointed steps. If they successfully meet all responsibilities, the judge will expunge their criminal charges.

The drug court graduation I was invited to holds a ceremony for all the people who have successfully completed the program. Graduates can invite their families to see their charges dropped and celebrate afterwards at a reception. During the graduation, the judge calls each graduation candidate, reads their charges, and then asks them what the greatest obstacle was in their recovery process. There were many touching stories of overcoming the loss of family, financial struggles and relational conflicts. Many of the candidates realized their bad decisions were their responsibility.

However, other candidates stood up and expressed their frustration with the court, the judge, their families, and anyone else within fingers reach. They blamed their parents for not raising them well. They cited their parents' addiction issues as the source of their failures. They criticized the court for putting undue pressure on them through the drug court program instead of just throwing them in prison. They viewed the judge as someone who was trying to hurt them, rather than someone who was helping them.

As I listened to each person's story, I began to notice an alarming pattern. The people who were playing the blame game had all been in the process far longer than those who had taken responsibility for their actions. For some, it was years longer! Those who took responsibility for their actions and desires were able to break the cycle of addiction and failure, while those who did not take responsibility for their actions continued to struggle in the same unhealthy, negative cycle. They remained victims instead of becoming victors.

The Poison of Pride

Why do people fall into a victim mentality? Pride. **Pride neglects responsibility and shifts blame.** In its simplest definition, pride is thinking more highly of ourselves than we ought (Romans 12:3). This is why people blame God for all the evil in the world but don't give Him credit for the good we enjoy. We ask God "Why?" when a loved one gets cancer or passes away, but we don't ask God "Why?" when we are blessed to have them in our life to begin with. We even believe that if we removed certain variables from our lives and situations, then we would be victorious, successful and prosperous. So are you ready to take a pride test? Answer the questions below with total honesty.

- Do you believe you would be more successful if you could remove certain people from your life?

- If you could go back and choose your parents or family, do you feel you would be better off today?

We don't like to admit it, but many of us believe deep down that our lives are byproducts of our circumstances, rather than our decisions. More often than not, God gets the finger pointed at him for the cause of universal pain and suffering, as well as our personal pain, suffering and failures. I have had many conversations with people who reject God because they blame Him for their problems and pain. Some even go so far to say they don't believe in God because of their life experiences. In these situations I find myself thinking, "Really? You don't believe in God, but you still blame Him?" How is that even possible? Perhaps it is more accurate to say these people believe in God, they just don't like Him.

When we experience life's storms and battles, it is to our benefit to correctly diagnose what we are actually going through. If we continually revert back to an immature victim mentality and believe that everything is God's fault, we actually isolate ourselves from our help. It is very difficult to receive God's help and reject Him at the same time.

We all have been around people, maybe you are one of them, that when they fall into temptation they blame God. They blame their failures on God's choice to withhold His ability instead of looking at their side of the equation. Now we all know that most people won't actually come out and say that it is God's fault. We have learned to use religious and spiritual language to make ourselves sound good and feel better in our failures. It's amazing how we can make eating in the pig sty sound like we are walking the red carpet at a Hollywood event. **The reason we do this is because we love our image more than our purpose.**

The Purpose of Trials are to Move You Into God's Will

I hate to break this to you. Well, actually I don't. Everything that happens to you is not God's fault. Yes, God may allow things to happen, but He allows them to happen for a greater purpose, or because we have given permission for those things to happen. Every believer will face trials in their life. Trials are part of our maturing, trusting and growth process as disciples.

Peter shares this with us in 1 Peter 4:12-13: *"Beloved, do not be surprised at the fiery trial when it comes upon you to test you, as though something strange were happening to you. But rejoice insofar as you share Christ's sufferings, that you may also rejoice and be glad when his glory is revealed."*

Peter is telling us not to be surprised by trials. They are not a strange event for the believer. In fact, we should expect trials to be an ongoing occurrence in our lives. It is not a matter of *if* trials will come, but *when*. Trials can come in the form of persecution from non-believers and yes, even believers. They can come through sickness and disease, emotional upheavals, financial setbacks, and other situations. However, our trials are not without purpose. God often uses trials to produce something greater in our lives. In the previous passage, Peter states that our trials will produce a reason to rejoice and bring gladness into our lives. Yes, God will allow trials to come into our lives to move us deeper into His will, strengthen our faith, and bring the rewards He longs to give us. **Trials are instruments of God's blessings and promotion.** So if you are going through a tough season, cheer up, it may be that God is allowing your faith to be tested to see if you can handle more of what He has in store for you.

Sowing and Reaping is Living with the Consequences of Your Decisions and Actions

While everyone will go through trials in life, not everything we go through is a trial. **Your current obstacles, pain and lack of purpose may not have anything to do with God or the enemy. You may simply be reaping what you have sowed.** I know the idea of reaping and sowing is not popular with our culture's love affair with life coaches, self-help and Oprah theology, but you cannot reason away the principle of sowing and reaping. It is integral to all of creation. The principle of sowing and reaping is as applicable to gardening as it is to your life. Its effect is seen in both the physical and spiritual realm. Make no mistake about it. You will reap what you sow.

> *"Do not be deceived: God is not mocked, for whatever one sows, that will he also reap. For the one who sows to his own flesh will from the flesh reap corruption, but the one who sows to the Spirit will from the Spirit reap eternal life."*
> **Galatians 6:7-8 (ESV)**

Yes, I will say it. You probably got your DUI because you were drinking and driving, not because the enemy is after you! You probably got divorced because you let lust settle in your heart, and you sowed seeds of adultery through text messages, inappropriate conversations, and a lack of honor and love for your spouse - not because God is testing you!

The Purpose of Temptations

Temptations are eerily similar to trials but differ in their root cause and their objective. Temptations come to both the believer and non-believer. They are an instrument of Satan to move us out of God's will. He will try to convince us or deceive us into choosing our own way instead of God's way. **Where trials are an instrument of God, temptations are an instrument of Satan. Where trials are designed to get us into God's will, temptation is designed to get us out of God's will.**

Although temptations may look and feel like trials, they are very different. One of the problems with immature believers is that they may be going through a season of temptation and confuse it with a trial. This sounds like a minor misperception, but it can have disastrous results. Many people have been tempted and mistakenly believe that God is trying to test them. How can you determine if what you are going through is a trial, a temptation, or a time of reaping what you have sown? You can ask yourself a few questions:

- Am I faithfully following Jesus?
- Can what I am going through produce godliness in me and others?
- Is what I am going through producing greater trust in God or is it making me doubt God?
- Is what I am going through directly connected to a past decision or action I have made in my life?

The reason we want to think that our temptations are trials is so we can shift the blame to God, play the victim, and give ourselves a promise to hold onto instead of looking at ourselves as the real cause of our temptation. Many of us deal with the same temptations over and over again because we refuse to get to the root cause of our struggle. We get caught up in the blame game where we blame God or Satan and refuse to look at the role we play in our predicament. The enemy will always use our own desires to tempt us. I need you to hear this: **God is not your tempter. He is your deliverer.** He cannot be both.

Misdiagnosis

The enemy thrives when we misdiagnose the season we are in. He has you right where he wants you once you're convinced your trial is from God's desire to move you into His will. In reality, you may be reaping the seeds of disobedience, rebellion, and unwise decisions, but because you think it's God's will, you will never change or identify the weeds in your life that need uprooting. On the other hand, if you are in a trial God wants to use to purify your faith and move you deeper into His will, but you believe the enemy is tempting you, then you will forfeit the opportunity God has granted you to grow and move forward.

To succumb to sin is to reject God's will, and you become bitter and blame God, using your sin as a religious weapon and an excuse to continually fall for the enemy's tactics always remember:

- The purpose of trials is to strengthen you and move you deeper into God's will.

- The purpose of temptation is to weaken you and move you out of God's will.

- Sowing and reaping are your decisions and actions catching up with you.

4
Desires

We can only hope for what we desire.
C.S. Lewis

Desire is an innate part of life. As soon as we are born, we begin pursuing the fulfillment of our natural desires. Even before we are born, our desires are fulfilled through a symbiotic relationship with our mother, who meets our need for food and water by eating for two. Obviously, this is where we develop our insatiable need for ice cream and pickles! In the beginning, our mothers also fulfill our desire for connection and intimacy through perpetual closeness. A baby expresses his needs and realizes his desires by crying out to his mother to fulfill them. It is the beginning of a lifelong pursuit of the fulfillment of desires, and like a child, our desires continue to grow as they are expressed and realized.

Desire is an abstract concept. Ambiguous and intangible, it is not a word that is readily illustrated since everyone associates it with something different. The Oxford Dictionary defines desire as "A strong feeling of wanting to have something or wishing for something to happen." It's synonyms include words like passion, want, need, ambition, aspiration, craving and hunger. All of us are born with strong feelings of wanting something and looking for certain things to happen in our lives.

Desires can take many directions, but their roots are found in our hearts, souls, minds and bodies. Each of these four areas of our being have deep-rooted desires that seek to be expressed and fulfilled. From birth till death, we long for our desires to be understood and met through our relationships and choices. When they are fulfilled, we are content and happy. When they are unfulfilled, we become frustrated and look for ways to express our frustration. Sometimes we don't even know how to express our desires, and this, too, leads to frustration. Unexpressed desire always leads to unfulfilled desire, which in turn leads to frustration. When this happens, we live unfulfilled lives because the desires of our heart, soul, mind and body are unexpressed and unfulfilled.

Our Lives Are Led By Our Desires

Our desires color how we see the world and determine how we make decisions, which relationships we pursue, and the way we think. Ultimately, our desires lead us in the direction of our destinies. This is one of the reasons why Jesus answered the Pharisees so succinctly when they asked Him which one of all the commandments was the greatest.

> And one of the scribes came up and heard them dis-
> puting with one another, and seeing that he [Jesus]
> answered them well, asked him, "Which commandment
> is the most important of all?" Jesus answered, "The most
> important is, 'Hear, O Israel: The Lord our God, the
> Lord is one. And you shall love the Lord your God with
> all your heart and with all your soul and with all your
> mind and with all your strength.' The second is this:
> 'You shall love your neighbor as yourself.' There is no
> other commandment greater than these."
> **Mark 12:28-31 (ESV)**

In this passage, Jesus is saying that we are not led by rules. We are led by desire. In fact, the original Greek words for "heart, soul, mind, and body" all reference desire in their definitions. Here, Jesus is saying that if we correctly identify those desires and point them in the right direction for fulfillment, then all the other commandments will be fulfilled. What are the desires Jesus points out? The desires of our heart, soul, mind and body. He is saying that when we pursue a relationship with our Creator first, then God will fulfill all our desires. Every single desire we have can find its fulfillment in God and His purposes. He is also saying that these desires are what lead our lives, so we need to make sure that we are being led in the right direction.

We are born with a desire for eternity in our hearts. This means we carry with us an eternal longing and understanding of eternity that is rarely understood or expressed. Even King Solomon, who had immense amounts of riches and fame, expressed his unfulfilled desires for eternal knowledge and understanding. He states in **Ecclesiastes 3:11 (ESV)**, "He has made everything beautiful in its time. Also, he has put eternity into man's heart, yet he cannot find out what God has done from the beginning to the end." Here, he describes our eternal longing for an intimate and knowledgeable relationship with God. It is the very definition of desire - that strong feeling of wanting something and hoping for something in the future that is eternal. All of us are created with eternal desires that reside deep within our hearts. These desires lead our thinking, decision-making, and life's pursuits. The Apostle Paul describes our eternal longing this way:

> *"For I consider that the sufferings of this present time are not worth comparing with the glory that is to be revealed to us. For the creation waits with eager longing for the revealing of the sons of God. For the creation was subjected to futility, not willingly, but because of him who subjected it, in hope that the creation itself will be set free from its bondage to corruption and obtain the freedom of the glory of the children of God. For we know that the whole creation has*

been groaning together in the pains of childbirth until now. And not only the creation, but we ourselves, who have the firstfruits of the Spirit, groan inwardly as we wait eagerly for adoption as sons, the redemption of our bodies. For in this hope we were saved. Now hope that is seen is not hope. For who hopes for what he sees? But if we hope for what we do not see, we wait for it with patience." **Romans 8:18-25 (ESV)**

You are not alone. All of creation is longing for the eternal desires deep inside to be revealed and realized on the outside. We want to know eternity and understand it completely. We long to know our Creator and have a relationship with Him. We are driven to seek to fulfill these eternal desires. They are the foundation of our hope. This is why C.S. Lewis said, ""We can only hope for what we desire.[4]" Our hope for tomorrow is rooted in our eternal desire to connect with God. When we realize this desire, it gives way to hope, which gives us the strength to persevere through temporal pains, obstacles and suffering. God places eternity in our hearts to create a longing for Him and His Kingdom so that we have the hope we need to persevere as we face the struggles of this temporal world.

Life's Four Big Questions

We can summarize our eternal desires by answering what Christian apologist, Ravi Zacharias calls, "Life's Four Big Questions." The topics of the four questions are origin, meaning, morality and destiny, and all are rooted in our eternal desire to know and be known by God.

Origin asks: "Where do I come from? Who created me? What is my existence?"

Everyone wants to know their origin. Atheists and scientists attempt to answer questions of origin through theories such as the Big Bang or evolution. Christians find the answers to origin in God.

Meaning asks: "Why was I created? Why do I exist? Why am I here?"

Everyone wonders why they were created. We long to discover our purpose and live it out.

Morality asks: "What's right? What's wrong? What is justice?"

Everyone has a conscience. We all long to see justice expressed and realized.

Destiny asks: "Where am I going? Where is eternity?"

Everyone longs for direction and a destination. We want to understand the eternity God has placed in our hearts and see it realized.

All eternal desires and questions are answered in fulfilling the greatest commandment, which is to love God first and foremost with all that is in you. God put these questions in our hearts to create a desire in us to seek Him for the answers. He is ready, willing and waiting to answer the longings of our hearts.

He answers the questions of your origin in his Word when he declares that you are not an accident or the byproduct of your family. He knew you before you were in your mother's womb, and He created you in His image.

> *"For you formed my inward parts;*
> *you knitted me together in my mother's womb.*
> *14 I praise you, for I am fearfully and wonderfully made.*
> *Wonderful are your works;*
> *my soul knows it very well.*

15 My frame was not hidden from you,
when I was being made in secret,
intricately woven in the depths of the earth.
16 Your eyes saw my unformed substance;
in your book were written, every one of them,
the days that were formed for me,
when as yet there was none of them.
17 How precious to me are your thoughts, O God!
How vast is the sum of them!
18 If I would count them, they are more than the sand.
I awake, and I am still with you." **Psalms 139:13-18**
(ESV)

"Before I formed you in the womb I knew you,
and before you were born I consecrated you;
I appointed you a prophet to the nations." **Jeremiah 1:5**
(ESV)

"But when he who had set me apart before I was born,
and who called me by his grace." **Galatians 1:15 (ESV)**

"And now the Lord says,
he who formed me from the womb to be his servant,
to bring Jacob back to him;
and that Israel might be gathered to him—
for I am honored in the eyes of the Lord,
and my God has become my strength." **Isaiah 49:5 (ESV)**

Meaning

He answers the questions of meaning by stating that everything He creates is designed to fulfill His eternal purpose. He has created you with a purpose, gifted you with gifts of His Spirit, and allowed you to have life experiences that are all part of your living out your purpose on earth before you spend eternity with Him in heaven. He even guides and leads you with His Spirit to discover and fulfill your eternal purpose. **(Jeremiah 29:11-14; Ephesians 2:10; 2 Timothy 3:17; Hebrews 13:21)**

Mortality

He answers the questions of morality by revealing truth to you and allowing His Spirit to convict you of any wrongdoing and encourage you to keep on doing what is right. He also promises us that eternal justice will be realized by all of us at the end of time. **(John 16:13; Isaiah 30:18; Psalm 9:7-8; Acts 10:34-35)**

Destiny

He answers the questions of destiny by giving us the promise of eternal life in His Son, Jesus. You don't have to wonder where you will go after you die, or what it will be like. God fulfills our desire for an eternal destiny by preparing a place for everyone who is born again in Jesus. In heaven, the eternity that God placed within our hearts is fully realized. **(John 3:16; John 14:3; 1 Corinthians 2:9; Hebrews 13:14)**

Fulfillment

God wants us to find the fulfillment of our hearts in Him and His love for us. He created us with this desire to know Him and to be known by Him. When Jesus said that loving God is the greatest commandment, it is a truth not rooted in a demand, but desire. God wants to be wanted. Christian author, A.W. Tozer said, "A woman doesn't want to be the object of duty; She wants to be desired. So does God."

> [*"God is a lover looking for a lover..."*
> **~ Misty Edwards, See The Way**]

God doesn't want to be the object of duty, just like a wife doesn't her husband to "have to" love her. Men, your wife wants you to pursue her and desire her. The old joke: "I told you I loved you when I married you and if that changes I'll let you know," does not satisfy her desire to be loved by you. This attitude doesn't work for God either. He wants to be desired. He wants to feel your love for Him every day, not just the day you got saved. He doesn't want religious affection, where loving Him is a club requirement. He wants to be pursued by people who are passionate about Him. He wants to be wanted.

God created us with the desire to know Him, but He leaves what we do with that desire up to us. This is the crux of free will. He created us and longs to have a relationship with us, but he also gives us the freedom to choose how we fulfill the deep desires He gave us — all the while knowing we may not even want Him. That is reckless love. His love creates, risks and sacrifices itself without any guarantee of love being returned.

God wants "all" of our heart, not just parts of it. He is a jealous God. **He is not jealous *of* anyone or anything else we may use to fulfill our desires. He is jealous *for* us.** He knows that we are led by our desires and that He is the only one that can fulfill them in a positive, healthy, holy and eternal way. He wants what is best for us. You may be thinking your whole heart is a lot for God to ask, but I personally think He is not asking enough. He gave everything He had for us, and even His request that we die to ourselves is rooted in His unending love and concern for our wellbeing.

God Created Us With An Immortal Soul

The soul is the center of our consciousness, and where we process our emotions and desires. The Greek word for soul is *psychi*, and it is the root for the English word psyche, which is defined by *Strongs Greek* as breath or breath of life. The soul is where we contemplate life, feelings and desires. It is where we dream and wonder. God created us with a soul because we are made in His image and God has a soul. He has an eternal consciousness. He has emotions and desires.

God knows that our soul's desire finds its expression and fulfillment in loving Him, and Him alone. When God is the object of our worship, our souls find the ideal place to express our longings, sorrows, griefs, joys, excitement and other emotions. Worship and prayer enable us to connect with God, express our hearts, and realize the intimacy we so desperately long to have with our Creator.

All of our souls' desires and emotions can and should be fulfilled in Jesus. He created us with emotions to help us search for, connect with, and worship God. It is when we allow these desires to lead us in a direction away from God's that we get into trouble. When our souls attempt to fulfill desires apart from God, we find emptiness and frustration, not fulfillment.

God Has a Mind, and He Created Us With a Mind

Everyone has a mind even if they don't use it. God's mind thinks thoughts that are higher than our thoughts. He has thoughts about you, your life and your family. He has thoughts about me, too. His mind is brilliant, creative, artistic and logical. When God created us in His image He gave us a mind that is creative, artistic and logical, just like His.

God gives us minds, so that we may pursue knowledge and truth, as well as the source of all knowledge and truth — God Himself. Our minds process all of our thoughts, memories and desires as we seek to understand the world around us. The pursuit of knowledge, truth and understanding begins at birth. Children are eager to experience their "new world," and it is a delight to watch them process their surroundings - from the wonder they express the first time they touch something, like soft green blades of grass, to the unbridled thrill they share when experiencing a new activity, like splashing water in the tub. We love witnessing these events - that is until our kids can walk and their desire to understand the world around them causes complete chaos. Hello, terrible twos!

A few years ago, my wife and I had four children under the age of four. One day, she needed to run to the store so she asked me if I thought I could watch all four kids by myself. I told her with great confidence, "I'm a dad. I can watch my own kids." She warned me, "Do not go to sleep!" Then, she left me with a four-year-old, two-year-old twins, and a one-year-old baby. I played with the kids for a minute and then my son, who was the baby, became tired and sleepy. Being a good dad, I placed him on my chest and laid on the couch so he could take a nap. That was the last thing I remember — until I heard my wife's car pull into the driveway. Her last words sprang to mind, "Do not fall asleep!" I jumped from the couch and ran around the house like a teenager whose out-of-town parents were back early and about to catch him hosting an epic party. To my credit, I was able to immediately locate all of my kids. However, when I found my two-year-old twin girls, they had been busy "doing their hair" and their little heads were covered in vaseline. It's important to note that when I say covered I mean completely drenched, saturated and coated in sticky, gooey, nasty vaseline!

For a moment, I thought about packing a bag, running out the back door, and escaping to a foreign country that does not extradite, but I didn't have time. My wife walked in the door, saw me and our two vaseline saturated twins and said, "You fell asleep, didn't you?" At first, I lied and told her, "I turned around for five minutes and these little unsanctified, unconverted heathens manifested with a jar of vaseline!" But she knew the truth. Mamas always know. Fortunately, after years of marriage counseling, parenting books and many cups of coffee I can say that our marriage is now healthy and vaseline has been banned as contraband in our house. Of course, the question remains, "Why would our girls do that?" They were trying to understand the world they live in. They were curious and wanted to know how to do their hair. You see, our minds have a desire to understand life. God gave us the desire to understand by seeking knowledge and truth. He gave us this desire because He knows that if we embrace it, it will lead us straight to Him.

God gives us minds that want to explore. Although we can never know everything about God and His mysterious ways, pursuing Him for understanding always brings us closer to His heart. It is the mystery of God that creates in us a holy curiosity that leads us to know Him more intimately. I once heard comedian Michael Jr. say, "If we could explain God, then He wouldn't be God." When God says that He wants us to love Him with all of our minds, He is really inviting us to embrace our holy curiosity and engage in a lifelong exploration of the mysteries of His mind and ways.

We Are to Love God With All Our Strength

Jesus says that we are to love God with all of our strength. The meaning of strength in the original language refers to ability, force or might. God expects us to express our love for Him through our natural ability and our physical bodies. He created our bodies as vessels to house our true self - our heart, mind and soul. He views the actions we take in our bodies as an expression of our true selves, for it is with our bodies and strength that we act upon our beliefs.

Although our bodies feature unique physical characteristics that distinguish us from one another on earth, those characteristics do not represent who we truly are. More importantly, God does not see us by our skin color, hair color, size, weight, or any other characteristic of our outer appearance. When the prophet Samuel was searching for the man God had chosen to be king over Israel, he assumed God had chosen David's brother Eliab because of his height and good looks. However, God told him, "Samuel, don't think Eliab is the one just because he's tall and handsome. He isn't the one I've chosen. People judge others by what they look like, but I judge people by what is in their hearts." **1 Samuel 16:7 (ESV)** God sees us for who we truly are. He sees our hearts, our minds and our souls.

Our bodies have desires for food, sex and comfort. The desire for food stirs up our ambition. We look for ways to earn money and produce wealth so that we can have enough food to eat and provide for our families. The desire for comfort increases our ambition. We strive to have more because we believe more wealth and more things produce more comfort. The desire for sex leads us to pursue marriage and family. These desires, when fulfilled by God, produce life.

As creatures of desire, God created us to be led by our desires directly into a rewarding and fulfilling relationship with Him. Contrary to what the world would have you believe, God wants to stir our desires, not suppress them. Religion suppresses desire with rules and regulations. Jesus stirs the desires within us by demonstrating His desire for us. Many of us have lost our desires because we have lost sight of God's desire for us. We need to recognize His great desire for and toward us and let that spark a revival of our desire for Him.

A Parable of Two Marriages

In his *Book of Illustrations*, Tony Evans captures the difference between religion and relationship through a parable about two marriages (excerpted below).

"There is a story of a woman who had a husband who kept a list. The list contained twenty-five things he wanted her to do in order to be a good wife for him. Every day he took out the list and he checked off the things that she completed. Cooking - check! Cleaning - check! Care of the kids - check! At the end of the day, he would let her know how she scored - twenty-three out of twenty-five. Twenty-one out of twenty-five, etc. This woman was miserable. She was miserable because she didn't marry to be tied to a checklist. Not that the things she did as a wife weren't important. They were important and they were necessary. But she had higher hopes for her marriage relationship.

After a number of years, the husband died. The woman felt a weight lifted from her shoulders because she had been performing for years. She had been doing her duty and hating every minute, even though the duties themselves weren't innately bad.

Two years later, this same woman fell in love with a new guy - a guy who had no lists. He told the woman that all he wanted to do was to love her. He wanted her to wake up in the morning knowing that he loved her. In the middle of the day, he wanted to be able to call and remind her that he loved her. At night, before they retired, he wanted to reassure her that he loved her. He wanted his love for her to be her every waking thought of her day. He wanted her to know his love, not his lists.

One day she was cleaning the house. She opened up a drawer and saw a piece of paper. It was the list from the first husband. She began to giggle when she realized that everything written down, all twenty-five duties, were happening effortlessly in her new marriage. Everything she had hated doing out of requirement by the husband, she was doing for the second husband - and loving it! All the second husband had was love. It brought joy to this woman, to her home, and all that she did for it. She was overpowered by love.[5]"

God Loved Us First

God desired us first and He seeks to ignite our desires for Him by demonstrating His immense love for us through Jesus' sacrificial death and resurrection. As Romans 5:8 states, "But God demonstrates his own love for us in this: While we were still sinners, Christ died for us." Think about that. Before you and I knew God, when we were unworthy sinners, who openly rebelled against Him, He desired to have a relationship with us. That is grace.

Carefully following rules, lists, and regulations does not produce godly desires or a right relationship with God. Godly desires are a by-product of His desire for us. We love Him because He first loved us (1 John 4:19). We pursue Him because He first pursued us. We serve Him because He first served us. It is God's unconditional love that produces in us the freedom and desire to love and serve Him.

> *"Or do you presume on the riches of his kindness and*
> *forbearance and patience, not knowing that God's*
> *kindness is meant to lead you to repentance?"*
> **Romans 2:4 (ESV)**

We are ultimately led to salvation not by fear, rules and failures, but by God's desire for us. He desires to save us so that we may be with Him. When our eyes are opened to this reality, we are led by His grace to accept the gift of salvation through His Son, Jesus. This is the beginning of a life led by God's desires.

The enemy knows it is God's desire to lead us by and fulfill the desires that He gave us. The enemy attempts to use our desires as the infrastructure and the bait of his tactics to move us out of God's will and disqualify us from His promises for our lives. There is a war that is raging right now over your desires. It is a real war with casualties, loss and death. The only question is: do you realize it?

5

Temptations

The problem with desire is, you want everything.
Paul Simon

"In the 1920s, a well-known, wealthy industrialist controlled a vast portion of our country's prosperity, and with his wealth he purchased a zoo. It wasn't a public zoo or even a private zoo; it was his personal zoo, located on his estate, for the pleasure of this one man and his family. National dignitaries were occasionally allowed to view the animals. In the days before zoo-breeding programs traded animals, his zoo was one of the most complete collections the zoological world had ever known. (During this time, zookeepers traveled to various countries, mounted safaris, and captured the animals to bring them back.)

One day he heard about a rare and beautiful type of gazelle from Africa that wasn't showcased in any zoo in the world. He became obsessed with the idea of becoming the first to have one of these animals in his collection.

He mounted an expedition to Africa, including food, supplies, and men to carry the tents. When they landed on the African shore, the man contacted the natives to learn about this animal and its whereabouts. Over and over he was told, "You'll never catch one. They're too fast and too strong. You can shoot and kill them from a distance—but you'll never get close enough to take one alive."

He told a reporter who was on the safari with him, "Don't listen to them; I'll get as many of them as I want! And it won't be a problem."

When his men located a herd, he poured sweet feed—a blend of oats and barley rolled in molasses—on the ground in an open area in the middle of the night and left. The next night he scattered the feed again. For two weeks, he spread the feed, night after night.

The animals, of course, came and ate it. On the first night of the third week, he scattered the feed and sank an eight-foot post into the ground twenty feet away. The next night, he scattered the feed and sank another post into the ground twenty feet in the opposite direction. Every night, he added a post. Then he started putting boards between the posts while scattering the feed.

Six weeks rolled by and he continued adding posts and boards until he had a corral built around the feed. Every night the animals found the gaps between the posts until, finally, he watched the entire herd squeeze through the last gap. Then he moved in behind them and nailed the last board into place. The animals were trapped inside the corral.

He chose the animals he wanted to take residency in his zoo and let the others go.

When he was asked how he knew how to catch them, his reply was chilling: "I treat animals the same way I treat people: I give them what they want. I give them food and shelter. In exchange, they give me their beauty and their freedom.⁶"

The Enemy Uses Your Desires Against You

The enemy is not going to tempt you away from God by using something you don't desire. His plan is to tempt you with something you desperately desire. Something for which you would sacrifice everything you have in order to attain it. Thus he will take something you want and will present it to you at your weakest, or perhaps even your most comfortable moment. But because you're dealing with the enemy, he is going to short-change you. **God wants to be the**

one to fulfill your desires. The enemy will offer you a cheap counterfeit at a more expensive price. It's not a matter of having our
desires fulfilled. It's a matter of how we choose to fulfill them.

> "Sin comes when we take a perfectly natural desire or
> longing or ambition and try desperately to fulfill it with-
> out God. Not only is it sin, it is a perverse distortion of
> the image of the Creator in us. All these good things, and
> all our security, are rightly found only and completely in
> him."
>
> - **Augustine, *The Confessions of Saint Augustine***

God gives us desires for love, intimacy, acceptance, belonging, provision, and even for sex. He also provides us with godly ways to fulfill
those desires. He gives us His Son to provide us with unconditional love,
acceptance, belonging and intimacy. He gives us marriage for intimacy
and sex. He gives us His church for acceptance and belonging. He gives
us jobs and health to provide for our needs. God wants to fulfill all of the
desires that He created in us. In fact, He gives us these desires to draw us
toward Him so that He can fulfill them.

Temptation comes when we begin pondering our desires, deciding
for ourselves how and when our desires should be fulfilled. Sin occurs
when we are deceived into believing our desires are not being fulfilled
by God, and so we make decisions without Him. This is how our enemy,
the serpent, tempted Adam and Eve in the Garden of Eden. He did not
tempt them with outright evil, but with something that appeared good.
In his book, *Tempted and Tried*, Russell Moore describes it this way:

> *"When the serpent attacked Eve, he did so by appealing to
> desires that God had created within her, desires that were,
> in and of themselves, like the rest of creation "very good."
> The snake knew not to question the goodness and sover-*

eignty of God outright, at first. Instead he let her ponder
what she wanted, and then ponder why she didn't have it.
He pulled her craving along to envy and her envy along to
action. Lured by her own desires, she became the serpent's
slave." [7]

When we start looking for ways to fulfill our desire instead of
looking to God, we're headed for grave disappointment. When
Adam and Eve sinned they were no longer looking for God. In fact,
they began hiding from Him. Their desire to seek after God and be
with Him had been exchanged for a desire to seek after themselves.

Can you imagine? In one moment they are seeking God. They have
everything they could ever need and everything they could ever want,
but it is not enough. They go from seeking God to hiding from God.
They go from loving God to loving godly stuff; from living freely out in
the open with no shame, to hiding from God and covering their shame.
I think it is safe to say that Adam and Eve were embarrassed by their
new desires. Their new desires told God that He was not enough to
fulfill them. He was not enough to love them. He was not enough to
satisfy them. I love what John Eldredge says about their experience:
"When we lived in Eden, there was virtually no restriction on pleasure
around us. We could eat freely from any tree in the garden. Our desire was innocent and fully satisfied. I cannot even imagine what five
minutes in total bliss would be like. We had it all, but threw it away. By
mistrusting God's heart, by reaching to take control of what we wanted,
Adam and Eve set in motion a process in our hearts, a desperate grasp-
ing that can be described only as addiction. Desire goes mad within us.
May observed, 'Once they gave in to that temptation, their freedom was
invaded by attachment. They experienced the need for more. God knew
that they would not - could not - stop with just the one tree.' "[8]

The enemy tempts us with our own desires. This is the point that James is trying to make to readers in James, chapter one. "Let no one say when he is tempted, I am being tempted by God, for God cannot be tempted with evil, and he himself tempts no one. But each person is tempted when he is lured and enticed by his own desire." (James 1:13-14, ESV). God is not tempting you. The enemy is. We are tempted by our own desires. That's right, your own desires, not someone else's. The enemy is going to tempt you with what you want or with what you believe you deserve.

The enemy knows what you desire and He is going to use that knowledge to sell you what you want at an extremely expensive rate. He is going to offer you your desires in a nice shiny package with a great sticker price. What he will not show you is the fine print. He will not show you the interest rate you will have to pay to finance your desires through him. He will not show you the finders' fee he charges for providing you with what you want. And believe me, he knows what you want.

Have you ever opened Netflix, Hulu or Youtube to watch a video and noticed how each of these media providers seem to know exactly what you are interested in? It is amazing how they not only know what I desire to watch, but fill my timeline full of content geared to my interests, while simultaneously eliminating content I'm not likely to watch. For instance, if you were to open my Hulu account, you would immediately be offered viewing options for sports, news, and Chip and Joanna Gaines shows — thanks to living with four women. Open my Youtube app and you will see a mixture of sports and FailArmy videos, documentaries, and old school preaching like Oral Roberts. Sometimes I will open Youtube and see a bunch of Fortnite videos, although I don't watch or play Fortnite because it is computer-generated crack straight from the pits of hell. So why would Fortnite videos show up in my timeline? Because my son has been logged in to my account watching Fortnite videos while he is grounded from playing the actual game.

How do Youtube, Hulu, and Netflix know what we desire to watch? They have incredibly intelligent mathematicians and programmers who create algorithms that learn what we like. These algorithms keep up with what we watch and how often we watch them. Then, these algorithms start running processes to find other videos that are similar to the ones we are already watching and they present them to us on our timelines. It makes our video viewing experience much easier and quicker when our experience is customized according to who we are and what we desire.

The enemy works just like Youtube, Hulu, and Netflix. No, he doesn't fill your life and mind with stupid cat videos and FailArmy compilations. He learns what you like and what you desire and then tempts you with what you want by continually placing it in front of you. His modus operandi is to get you to click play on your desires. To take the analogy even further think about when you visit YouTube. Most of the time we turn to YouTube to entertain us when we are inactive, bored or tired. Rarely (if ever) do we visit Youtube because we are actively pursuing our goals. It is when we are passive in our pursuit of God that the enemy will tempt us the most. These are the times when he bombards our thoughts with temptations. We open the YouTube app of our minds and our timeline is flooded with everything we want to see, have and do.

The enemy knows your greatest dreams and your most fearful nightmares. He knows your most holy desires and your most evil hidden desires. He knows the desires that you suppress, as well as the promises that God has given you that have yet to be fulfilled. More importantly, he will attempt to use all of this knowledge against you. He knows you are led by your desires and if he can entice you to fulfill those desires apart from God, he can lead you into sin, captivity, and ultimately death.

How We Are Tempted By Our Desires

The enemy tempts us by taking away something we desire or by giving us something we desire (that God promised us) through other means outside of God's will and ways. We see this in the story of Job. The enemy began by taking away his material blessings, including his family. I am sure Job loved his family and his desire was to be with them for their well-being. Where did the enemy try to tempt him? He tempted him at the root of his desires. What is your greatest desire that God has fulfilled in your life? Is it your family, marriage or kids? Is it your career or your retirement account? Is it your ministry, your church or simply your comfort? Whatever it is, be assured the enemy will use it to tempt you away from God's purpose and will for your life.

The enemy will also tempt us by using our desire for something we don't have, yet. It is usually something that God has promised us or something we feel we deserve or are entitled to. If you happen to feel entitled to God's blessings, let me encourage you to submit to some humble soul-searching. None of us deserves anything less than death and hell, BUT GOD, rich in mercy, has given us His gift of everything in Christ Jesus! The enemy's temptations thrive when there is a gap between what we desire and what we possess. He will tempt us into bitterness toward God for not fulfilling His promises or taking too long to fulfill them. He will tempt us to achieve our desires by circumventing God's plan and ways. He will tempt us to take control and recklessly follow our own path to satisfy our desires. What desires do you have that have yet to be fulfilled or satisfied? Is it a promise from God for a child? Is it for a godly spouse? Is it your husband or wife coming to salvation in Jesus? Or is it to see your children return to the Lord? Is it the ministry that God promised you? Is it to start a business that God put in your heart? Whatever your desire, be aware that the enemy is going to use it against you and against God.

Your desires are the tip of the spear in the enemy's arsenal for his attacks against you. Since we are creatures of desire he knows that our desires are the key to winning our attention, focus, faith and even our worship. We must become more aware of the desires that are rooted deep within our souls. We must admit what we want and why we want it. We have to pay attention to those desires for they will be the battlefield of our God-given purpose. You are a creature of desire and your desires will ultimately lead you to your destiny. Where are your desires leading you in your life right now?

6

Realization

If we confess our sins, he is faithful and just to forgive us our sins and to
cleanse us from all unrighteousness. If we say we have not sinned,
we make him a liar, and his word is not in us.
1 John 1:9-10 (ESV)

We must acknowledge our desires because they are also the source of our temptations. If you want to be victorious over your temptations, you have to know where the battle takes place. Having this information enables you to more effectively prepare for battle. The U.S. military trains specifically for the territory in which they believe their next battle will take place. If the next battle is in Iraq, our military trains soldiers in desert warfare. If the next battle is in Vietnam, our military trains soldiers in jungle warfare. If the next battle is in a major city, our military trains soldiers in urban warfare. The location of the battle often determines not only how we engage our enemy, but what weapons we must use to defeat him.

The battleground of your temptation is and will always be your desires. Fortunately, this means you know your battleground better than your enemy does. You are more familiar with the terrain, the layout and the obstacles. You know the hidden places and the open vulnerabilities. You have the advantage over the enemy because you are fighting from the high ground. In fact, you have what's called the home-court advantage.

When I was growing up I played basketball every single day, anywhere and everywhere there was a basketball goal. I played in local gyms with hardwood floors, at the park on a blacktop surface, and at homes with paved or gravel driveways. Nothing helps you to become a better ball handler then learning to dribble on different surfaces. My favorite court was the one at my house. It wasn't the best court, but it was mine. My dad and I installed the goal ourselves. Not an adjustable height goal that I could lower and practice dunking. I wish! And it didn't have a breakaway rim or a plexiglass backboard. It was simply a fiber-glass backboard with a standard rim mounted on a piece of pipe my dad brought home from work. The court wasn't concrete or blacktop. It was dirt. There were no free throw or three point lines. Even so, I loved my court, because on my court I had home-court advantage. I knew the details, obstacles, flaws and nuances of my court how the ball was going to bounce off the rim or roll off the backboard as well as all the spots where the ball wouldn't dribble as true as it would on hardwood.

Your Home-Court Advantage

You have a home-court advantage against the enemy when you acknowledge your flaws and your desires. The Bible says in 1 John 1:9, "If we confess our sins, he is faithful and just to forgive us our sins and to cleanse us from all unrighteousness." That means we have an advantage when we acknowledge our shortcomings. Our relationship with Jesus begins by acknowledging our sins and failures to God in order to attain the victory of salvation. In the same way, we maintain our victory and move from glory to glory by continuing to acknowledge our desires so that God can help us overcome them.

In order for you to have home-court advantage, you need to recognize the flaws and obstacles you have in your life. You must acknowledge the desires you have that the enemy can use to lure you away from your relationship with God. As I stated earlier, your desires are where the enemy will engage you in battle. For where your desires are the strongest, there you will face your greatest temptations. The enemy will use your past sins, failures and passions to tempt you to sin and draw you away from God's promises. Have you ever noticed that every time you make a decision to grow or move forward in your walk with God, the enemy brings up your past sins and failures? He does this to make you feel unworthy of following or serving Jesus. Thank God Jesus is the God of today and tomorrow, not our past! The enemy wants us defeated by our past and burdened with the mindset of a sinner, instead of the victorious mindset of a child of God.

The enemy will use your former passions and desires before you were saved to tempt you when you are saved! As a matter of fact, **your primary area of sin before you got saved will probably be your primary area of temptation after you get saved.** If you were a sexual person before you were saved, you are probably going to deal with sexual temptation. If you were an angry person before you got saved, you are probably going to be tempted with anger. On that note, if anger is your weakness, you should probably avoid rush hour traffic, Black Friday shopping sprees, and all political discussions. If you dealt with addictions before you got saved, you will likely be tempted by addictions and their habits afterward. Why? Because the enemy knows that you already have a deep desire for those things. Why try and get you to develop new desires when he can simply stir up your old ones? He will bring up memories of the "good ole days" before you were saved to stir your emotions and feelings of shame. Whether he stirs up old desires to tempt you or haunts your thoughts with past shame, his goal is to make you feel unworthy of God's grace and love.

Before I was saved, I lived a terrible life filled with anger, sexual promiscuity, drugs and alcohol. Out of all those things, sexual promiscuity was the desire that had the greatest impact on my life. When I got saved, Jesus gave me a new heart and a new spirit, but He did not give me new flesh. I still had the same flesh that had run my life and dictated my decisions. Although Paul tells us in 1 Corinthians 2:14-16 that all believers have the mind of Christ, he also warns us in Romans 12:2 that we must renew our minds in order to have the life Christ died for us to have. That means it's our job to change our thought patterns. Although God had declared my mind was now Christ's territory, like the Israelites entering the Promised Land, I would need to actively take captive every thought, mental image and memory of sin and shame I had ever experienced. Being saved, it became very clear that my spirit and flesh were now at odds with one another, and I found myself engaged in an intense battle of desires. Just as we must take out thoughts captive, the Bible also tells us to crucify the flesh and its desires. God gives us a new spirit, but we are responsible for taking control of our mind and flesh. That is how we work out our salvation (Philippians 2:12).

Naturally, my past sexual promiscuity and the shame that came with it became an intense battleground the enemy used to tempt me. About 10 years ago, I received a life-changing letter. At this point in my life everything was going well. My marriage and family were a blessing. We had just bought a new home. Our finances and ministry were on solid ground, and the church where we were on staff was experiencing phenomenal growth. However, this letter was intended by the enemy to change all of that.

Now we are all used to getting advertisements and bills in the mailbox, but this letter looked nothing like regular mail. In fact, it looked like something from a TV murder mystery, where words and letters cut from a magazine are pasted onto a sheet of paper forming a diabolical message. At first glance I thought, 'Is someone planning to kill me?' Looking back, I realize that thought was not far from the truth. In fact it seemed obvious to me at the time that the enemy intended to kill God's plan for my life.

As I read the letter, my entire past life, with all of its shame and guilt were brought into my new life with Christ. The letter, which was anonymous, was from a female I had known during my time in the military. She wrote the letter to let me know that she had just had a baby with her husband, but during the pregnancy they had diagnosed her as HIV positive. She mentioned that her husband and baby were negative. The intent of her letter was to accuse me of giving her the virus. She even mentioned that her father had told her not to hang around guys like me but she didn't listen, and now she had to deal with her situation the rest of her life, not knowing how long that would be.

My heart sank to the pit of my stomach, and I became overwhelmed by shame, guilt and fear. It was as if the enemy knew how well my life was going, now that I was walking out God's plan. So he decided to pay me a visit, to say "Remember me, old friend?" Although I hurt for this woman who had received such terrible news, I was also angry that she was pointing her finger at me; I was also terrified by the possibility I might be HIV positive, and that I might have infected my beautiful, pure wife and our precious children.

Everyone in our town knew me because I had grown up there. Moreover, our church was the most influential church in the city, so I couldn't casually drop by my doctor's office and get an HIV test. What would people think? I also didn't want to tell my wife without knowing if I was positive or negative. Alone, afraid and consumed by worry, I drove to another town and visited their health department where I asked for an HIV test, only to be told I would have to go to my doctor for one.

I called a doctor's office in another town and scheduled an appointment for an HIV test, conscious of the change in the receptionist's voice when I asked for the test. On the day of the test, I walked in cloaked in shame, took the test and was told I would know the results in 24 long, anxiety-ridden hours.

As I waited, I went about my normal routine. I worked at the church, visited people at the hospital and ate dinner with my family. Finally, the call came and I was told, "Your test results are negative."

My incredible relief lasted only a few minutes before the guilt set in. For I had lived the same kind of life the woman had, yet managed to escape the terrible consequences, while she had not. I wanted to make things right, to repair my past, but I couldn't. Why? My past had been washed in Christ's blood. I am a new creature in Christ. I have a new identity. There is nothing to repair. The enemy knew this, but he wanted to bring all the guilt, shame and consequences of the desires from my past into my new life to disrupt it. One of the greatest battles you will face is the temptation to bring your old life into your new life, your old identity into your new identity, and your old desires into your new ones.

I think many times we err in our thinking when it comes to being set free from sin. When we repent of our sin and make Jesus our Lord and Savior, our sins are instantly forgiven. However, **the enemy could not care less about your being forgiven. He remains your accuser, who is a deceiver and the enemy of your soul. He has not forgotten nor forgiven your sins.** When we are set free from sin, we are set free from the penalty of our sin, but not the memory of our sin. Thus, the enemy is going to use your memory of your past sins as the bait to attract you back into sin.

I recently had a conversation with an incredible young couple who were having some difficulties in their marriage. As we talked, the husband confessed to infidelity and homosexuality. He expressed his desire to be set free from homosexuality and to be a godly husband and father. I asked him what he thought being set free would look like. He stated that being set free would be freedom from the temptation. Wow! I wish we could all be set free from all of our temptations, but we will not see that day until Jesus returns! I lovingly told him that he may deal with same sex attraction or temptations his entire life because the enemy knows that having already experienced it, it's a viable temptation he will continue to   use to take him captive. You see, being set free is not being set free from temptation. Being set free is being able to acknowledge temptation and walk away from it rather than taking the bait and going back into bondage. Temptations will come, but recognizing the past consequences only makes it easier to walk away.

In his satirical book, The Screwtape Letters, C.S. Lewis writes a series of fictional letters from a senior demon named Screwtape to a junior tempter known as Wormwood, instructing him on how best to tempt people using their desires, past failures and shame. For a moment, let's take a cue from Lewis' book and play our own devil's advocate. If you were the devil, what desires would you use to tempt yourself? What old desires would you stir up? What memories, failures, or passions would you bring to mind in order to make you feel unworthy or ashamed? If you need help identifying your desires, below is a list of the 16 basic human desires chronicled by a noted scholar and clinical psychologist, Steven Reiss :

1. Power is the desire to influence others.
2. Independence is the desire for self-reliance.
3. Curiosity is the desire for knowledge.
4. Acceptance is the desire for inclusion.
5. Order is the desire for organization.
6. Saving is the desire to collect things.
7. Honor is the desire to be loyal to one's parents and heritage.
8. Idealism is the desire for social justice.
9. Social contact is the desire for companionship.
10. Family is the desire to raise one's own children.
11. Status is the desire for social standing.
12. Vengeance is the desire to get even.
13. Romance is the desire for sex and beauty.
14. Eating is the desire to consume food.
15. Physical activity is the desire for exercise of muscles.
16. Tranquility is the desire for emotional calm.[9]

As you consider which desires the enemy may use to tempt you and disrupt God's plan for your life, write them down so that you don't forget where your battle is. Then, find someone you trust and tell them what these desires are and how you believe the enemy will use them against you. You will need people to help you watch your blind spots. Next, set up boundaries and parameters to prevent yourself from being caught off-guard. I will go into more detail about protecting yourself from wrong desires later, but for now write your desires down, tell someone you trust and pray over your desires every day. Finally, always remember that your past does not define you. Your past has been placed in the grave with Christ, and you have been resurrected with Him to a new life and new identity.

Final Thoughts

We are led and tempted by desire. There is no freedom nor is there victory until you acknowledge your desires and acknowledge how the enemy will use your desires against you. Remember desires are natural and good. God is not anti-desire. God wants to fulfill your desires in a loving, eternal relationship with Him. In the next chapter we will discuss what to do with our desires and how to redirect them, but before we move forward ask yourself the question, "What sinful desires have I failed to acknowledge that the enemy is using to wreak havoc on my mind and heart through temptation?" Your freedom may be on the other side of that question. Once you acknowledge your desires you can correctly identify how the enemy will use your desires to disrupt God's plan for your life and correctly appropriate your desires for God's best good in your life.

7

Flesh

Watch and pray so that you will not fall into temptation.
The spirit is willing, but the flesh is weak.
Matthew 26:41 (NIV)

I haven't always been a preacher. In fact, far from it, which is why I don't always relate to many of my contemporaries who grew up in church, attended vacation Bible school and graduated from a private Bible college, their studies culminating at seminary. I grew up in what is considered a lower middle-class environment where I ran with the wrong crowd before joining the AirForce. Through the years I have seen my fair share of fights. I wish I could say that I won more than I lost, but the statistics of my fighting capabilities would deny me that privilege, which brings to mind one of my most embarrassing defeats.

It happened during homeroom in the seventh grade. Our teacher had left the classroom and another seventh grader began bullying one of the smaller students. Since our teacher was "missing in action", I decided to take control of the situation. So I got up and inserted myself between the two, and told him in the deepest voice I could muster to "cut it out!" But he wasn't the least bit intimidated by my deep voice or 90-pound frame and replied, "What are you gonna do about it?" In front of the entire homeroom class I let him know I would do plenty, and we began to push each other. Then, I hit him with my fist, expecting him to fall to the floor unconscious. Yet there he stood with a sinister smile on his face and the next thing I knew, I was on the floor while he repeatedly punched and kicked me. Finally our teacher returned to the classroom and pulled him off of me, and I got up crying (don't judge me) in front of the entire homeroom class.

Later that night I had a basketball game and played with a broken nose from my skirmish. Sure, I was defeated, but I was still tough. In fact my friend's mom recorded our game on their VHS camcorder and throughout the video you could hear parents commenting about my swelling nose that was growing bigger by the minute and turning every color of the rainbow!

My defeat was public because everyone involved in the school was aware of what had happened by word of mouth. However, when it comes to the struggles we face in our daily lives, the fight is rarely a public event. For most people the biggest battles are those fought in private, and although you may not have gone toe-to-toe with a bully, or thrown a punch, you have been in a fight. In fact, I guarantee you that you are in one right now.

Your Battle

There is a cosmic conflict taking place deep within your heart and mind. To be honest, your daily battle is much more than a fight. It is a war that has been going on since the creation of man. Its path of destruction has produced millions of casualties, destroyed families, wounded and killed innocent bystanders and obliterated countless destinies that could have brought glory to God and blessings to the world.

Think of your internal war like a presidential election. You have both sides of the aisle inside your soul. The debates are heated and go back and forth, campaigning against one another, making promises and using language directed to appeal to your desires. So who are the candidates? They are your flesh and God's Spirit. Your flesh and the Holy Spirit both want to be elected president of your life and the ruling force over your destiny. Your brain is constantly battling thoughts that each side presents to influence you. Like political ads, these thoughts draw your attention to how much better life will be if you choose one and not the other. Your heart is drawn to the promises each side makes as the two candidates attempt to motivate you to act on their guidance.

Your flesh and God's Spirit cannot rule together. They will never agree. Although they occupy the same space (your mind, heart, body and soul), they cannot get along. Compromise is never an option. Selfish and domineering, your flesh wants everything done its way — immediately. It is a slob that parties and indulges itself with whatever it wants. In the world of the flesh, you wake up to find empty pizza boxes on the table, drinks spilled all over the floor, and a random person in your bed. Your flesh does not care about anyone else, only itself. On the plus side, God's Spirit likes order. He is selfless and brings peace to every situation. He is the roommate that genuinely cares about you and is always looking out for your best interests and the interest of others.

Unfortunately, most people try to make the flesh and God's spirit co-presidents of their lives and end up living in a constant campaign mode. Could you imagine having to deal with a presidential campaign *every* year? I would move to Antarctica! That is what our lives are like when we try to make our flesh and God's Spirit equals in our lives.

The apostle Paul dealt with the same conflict in his soul that you may be dealing with. Here's how he described it:

> "So I find it to be a law that when I want to do right, evil lies close at hand. For I delight in the law of God, in my inner being, but I see in my members another law waging war against the law of my mind and making me captive to the law of sin that dwells in my members. Wretched man that I am! Who will deliver me from this body of death? Thanks be to God through Jesus Christ our Lord! So then, I myself serve the law of God with my mind, but

with my flesh I serve the law of sin." **Romans 7:21-25 (ESV)**

Paul realized that there was a genuine military campaign going on in his mind, heart, body and soul. He wanted to do right. He wanted to follow the right desires, but felt torn between the two. He cried out for help. John Piper gives us this encouragement, "The Spirit has landed to do battle with the flesh. So take heart if your soul feels like a battlefield at times."[10]

Have you ever cried out for help over your desire to please God and your desire to satisfy your flesh? If not, you have probably elected your flesh to be president of your life. You have no conflict because your flesh is governing your desires and your life, and ultimately, your destiny. If you have cried out, or feel that you need to, you are in a great place. I know the struggle is real, but the struggle means you are still pursuing God and want to honor Him.

Not content to leave us stranded in a war zone, Paul provides a solution to our inner battles in 1 Corinthians 15:57 (GWT), which says, "Thank God that he gives us the victory through our Lord Jesus Christ." We have victory over our internal conflicts through Jesus, who not only provides us with forgiveness of sins, but victory over all sin. He gives us a new nature through a new birth. Instead of just external forgiveness, Jesus provides us with internal transformation.

"Therefore, if anyone is in Christ, he is a new creation.
The old has passed away; behold, the new has come."
2 Corinthians 5:17 (ESV)

The Law and The Gospel

This verse demonstrates the key difference between the Law and the Gospel. The Law dealt with the external symptom of sin. It tried to clean up the mess of sin, but it could not give us power over sin because it could not make us new. The Law illustrates what holiness looks like, but it does not give us the ability to be holy. The Gospel gives us the ability to fulfill the Law. You see the Law is truth without power. The gospel is truth with power. This power is not just for forgiveness. It is power over sin.

The Gospel grants forgiveness of sin and provides us with power over sin and the flesh. In his book, The Normal Christian Life, author Watchman Nee illustrates a parallel between the blood of Jesus and the cross of Jesus. He creates a differentiation between sin and sins.

> *"It is because in the first section it is a question of the sins I have committed before God, which are many and can be enumerate [counted], whereas in the second it is a question of sin as a principle working in me...I need forgiveness for my sins, but I need also deliverance from the power of sin."*
>
> *- Watchman Nee*

The difference between sins and sin is clear. Your sins are those actions, decisions, and mistakes you have made against God, His will, His ways, His standard, and His Kingdom. They can be counted. They are tangible. You can make a list of them. You can confess them to a friend or a loved one. Your sin is the principle or the power of your sinful flesh in your life. Sin is not tangible. It is the desires and the passions of your flesh. You cannot count sin. You can feel its power. You can experience its grip. But you cannot count it. Sins are actions. Sins are actions. Sin is the power behind the actions.

Victory in Jesus

Here is the good news: Jesus brings victory for both. Watchman Nee says that the answer is found in the blood of Christ and the cross of Christ. The blood of Christ washes away your sins. The blood brings forgiveness of sins. It is the perfect blood of the Lamb that provides the necessary sacrifice and payment for our sins. The blood of Jesus satisfies the eternal debt for our sins that we could not pay on our own. THERE IS POWER IN THE BLOOD OF JESUS! It is powerful enough to remove your past sins, your past mistakes, your past failures, and your past life. It makes all things new!

> *"For all have sinned and fall short of the glory of God, and are justified by his grace as a gift, through the redemption that is in Christ Jesus, whom God put forward as a propitiation by his blood, to be received by faith. This was to show God's righteousness, because in his divine forbearance he had passed over former sins. It was to show his righteousness at the present time, so that he might be just and the justifier of the one who has faith in Jesus."*
> **Romans 3:23-26 (ESV)**

> *"But God shows his love for us in that while we were still sinners, Christ died for us. Since, therefore, we have now been justified by his blood, much more shall we be saved by him from the wrath of God."*
> **Romans 5:8-9 (ESV)**

The Way of the Cross

The blood of Christ takes care of my sins. The cross of Christ deals with the sinner. Nee says, *"The blood procures pardon for what we have done, the Cross procures our deliverance from what we are."* The blood of Christ fulfills God's requirement for a sacrifice to forgive sin. The cross is for my deliverance.

Just like we have to apply the blood of Jesus to our lives through repentance and believing in Jesus as our Lord and Savior, we must also apply the cross to our lives. How do we apply the cross? It is not by wearing one around your neck or hanging a crucifix above your doorpost, nor is having a beautiful cross in your sanctuary at church a means of application. No, the cross is a about crucifying a person. The cross is about death. It is not beautiful. It is gory and difficult to see. It is even harder to endure.

We apply the cross of Christ to our lives by allowing ourselves, the sinner, to be crucified along with Jesus. You see, you can be forgiven of your sins through the blood of Jesus, but you will never experience the power over sin and the freedom that Jesus has promised you without crucifying yourself. Your victory over your internal conflict comes from the cross, not the blood. Victory is yours through the cross of Christ! When you learn to crucify yourself and your fleshly desires, you will begin to walk in the freedom Jesus has promised you.

The problem with crucifixion is that it is not an enjoyable experience. It is not pleasant to place yourself upon a cross to die. Just like Jesus, it will take your submission to God and obedience to His will for you to face your own crucifixion. Jesus fought His flesh in the Garden of Gethsemane the night before He was crucified. He battled His flesh through prayer. You, too, will have to battle through prayer to obey God's will and crucify your flesh. Jesus was mocked for being crucified. You, too, will be mocked. Religious people will call you a radical. They will say things like, "You don't have to go that far. Just go to church and try to live a good life." They won't understand that your cross is your victory. We need forgiveness, yes, but we also need deliverance. Just like Jesus, crucifixion will be a painful experience that you will have to endure. Your flesh will get mad when you try to crucify it. Be prepared for pain, but let your pain point to your purpose. Your victory over your sinful, fleshly desires will be through the crucifixion of yourself.

Look at what Jesus said about taking up your cross:

> *Then Jesus told his disciples, "If anyone would come after me, let him deny himself and take up his cross and follow me. For whoever would save his life will lose it, but whoever loses his life for my sake will find it."* **Matthew 16:24-25 (ESV)**

Look at what Paul says about crucifying yourself:

> *"For if we have been united with him in a death like his, we shall certainly be united with him in a resurrection like his. We know that our old self was crucified with him in order that the body of sin might be brought to nothing, so that we would no longer be enslaved to sin. For one who has died has been set free from sin."* **Romans 6:5-7 (ESV)**

Paul is doing nothing more than teaching us what Jesus taught and gave Him. Your life, your abundant life of victory and freedom is found through crucifying yourself. Your victory is found through the cross of Jesus. You must crucify your flesh in order for the life of the Holy Spirit to reign in you.

Paul teaches us how to navigate our inner conflict of desire in Galatians, chapter five. Here, he shows us what he has learned in order to defeat the flesh and allow God's Spirit to rule our life and bodies. Your flesh will not go down without a fight. You must crucify it.

> *For you were called to freedom, brothers.*
> *Only do not use your freedom as an opportunity*
> *for the flesh, but through love serve one another.*
> **Galatians 5:13 (ESV)**

We were called to freedom in Christ. Before salvation, we were ruled by our flesh and its desires. We did whatever our flesh wanted and lived with the consequences. Through the Gospel of Jesus we are given freedom from our sins. What is sad is that many believers use the precious blood of Jesus and His amazing grace to satisfy themselves. They are self-centered. They only love God for what He can do for them. They use His grace as an excuse to sin and abuse His loving nature.

This shows us that the flesh is still active after salvation. When you say yes to Jesus, your sins are forgiven, but your flesh will need to be conquered. This is why Paul encourages us to crucify our flesh. Quick question. Have you said yes to Jesus but are still saying yes to your flesh? A yes to Jesus is a no to your flesh! Therefore, your victory may be on the other side of what you say yes and no to.

8

Crucifixion

*And those who belong to Christ Jesus have crucified
the flesh with its passions and desires.*
Galatians 5:24 (ESV)

For many years, I was in top shape physically and would regularly max out my physical training scores in the Air Force. I would hit the gym every day and sometimes twice a day. I spent a ton of money on supplements, vitamins and protein powders to help me build mass on my chicken-legged frame. I enjoyed working out and improving my overall health and look.

As time moved forward, I got married and we had one baby, then twins, and then a fourth baby. My gym life evolved from hitting the weights to chasing babies and changing diapers. I would go to the gym sporadically whenever I had a free moment, or when I had gotten all gung-ho and made a new year's resolution to get rid of my dad-bod.

Four years ago, my family and I moved from Nashville to Alabama, where about once a month, I would tell myself I was going to get back into a fitness routine, only to fail over and over. I did join a gym and regularly paid dues. I drove by the gym every single day, sometimes multiple times a day, but rarely did I enter its doors. A few weeks ago, I met a man at church and asked him what he did for a living and he said he ran the gym down the street. Uh oh, I thought, he was referring to my gym. I told him I was a member of his gym. Later that week I received an email with a subject line that said, "5 Times Really, Pastor Bobby...

Really?" I was busted. Yes, I was a member of the gym and I had access to everything I needed to get healthy and improve my physical life, but it was up to me to actually do it.

In much the same way, you and I have been given membership into God's family and Kingdom. Our membership is paid in full by Jesus, and He has granted us unrestricted, 24-hour access to everything we need. All the resources, power, and opportunities essential to our health and spiritual welfare are readily available, but it is up to us to follow-through and apply His power and resources to our lives. We will not become spiritually strong and healthy just by becoming members of the Kingdom of God. God gives us access, but we must get up and work-out in order to crucify our flesh and strengthen our spirit. Our flesh will not crucify itself.

The cross is your doorway and also the pathway to victory over your sin. **You are not given a new flesh when you are saved. It has to be crucified. It will not crucify itself. You will have to do it, and it will fight you every step of the way!** It will lead you to imagine you are going to die, and this is partially true. Part of you will die when you crucify your flesh, but it is the part that is holding you back from receiving God's crown of life!

Fasting

What does it mean to crucify your flesh? It means you suppress the desires of your flesh so that God's Spirit can be the most influential voice in your life. One of the greatest (and most overlooked) methods of crucifying your flesh is fasting. Fasting is forsaking fleshly desires for a season of time to focus on God's desires for you, His voice, and His direction for your life. Fasting in a sense is telling your flesh no for an extended amount of time. Fasting is putting your flesh in its rightful place of submission in your life.

All of the desires of your flesh are natural, including sex, honor, independence and eating. However, of all the desires your flesh has, eating is the most natural. Your body wants to eat, and if it is like mine, it wants to eat ice cream and a lot of it. Your flesh desires food to feed it. It is a strong desire that fights for attention. As a matter of fact, your flesh will talk to you. It will tell you what it wants. It will tell you that it wants ice cream when you pass Dairy Queen. It will tell you it wants coffee when you pass Starbucks. It will tell you it wants sex. It will tell you it wants revenge.

If eating is your strongest fleshly desire, then fasting makes sense. If you can tell your flesh no for an extended amount of time, you can train it to submit to your spirit. As you bring your flesh into alignment with your spirit, you can rule over it instead of allowing it to rule over you. Think about it. If you can get your flesh to submit to your spirit regarding food, its strongest, most basic desire, you can tell your flesh no when it comes to alcohol, tobacco, sex, anger, addiction, and all of its other desires. For those fighting addiction, fasting is a great way to crucify your addicted flesh. Remember, your spirit is free. It is your flesh that is addicted. Fasting is training your flesh to submit to your spirit. When your spirit is in charge, your life will reflect its freedom.

Just as your flesh is always speaking, God is, too. He wants your attention. While your flesh will scream at you, God whispers gently. Sometimes our flesh is so loud that it is difficult to hear or discern what God is saying. Fasting pretty much tells your flesh, "Shut up!" It removes all of the influences and stimuli in your life so that the voice of God is the only one left. Different types of food stimulate your mind and body, such as sugar, caffeine, alcohol and drugs. Radio and social media also stimulate your mind and body. When we fast, we remove the stimulants in our lives, except for the Spirit of God.

I personally believe that fasting can bring healing to our bodies because it enables them to function the way God designed them to. When we remove all of the processed food, chemicals and stimulants for a period of time, our bodies experience a cleansing and renewal that comes from eliminating toxins and operating in a more natural state. God created our bodies to heal themselves, and they do this best when they are empowered to function as God intended.

Renewing Your Mind

Another way to crucify your flesh is to actively and perpetually renew your mind. Your mind will not renew itself. It has been trained by the world, your flesh, and your life experiences to think a certain way. You will have to reformat it. Allow me to illustrate. If you have a computer that is not functioning correctly there could be something wrong with the operating system. It may be evident by Microsoft Windows' notorious 'Blue Screen of Death' or Apple's 'Spinning Beachball of Death.' Both are a sign that the operating system has an error or a bug. In order to resolve the issue, you will probably have to reformat the hard drive. You will have to remove the old operating system and install a new one. After you reformat the hard drive, your computer should operate correctly.

As the operating system of your body that processes thoughts, decisions, memories and ideas, your mind is like a computer hard drive, and like any computer, it requires regular updates, reformats and virus protection. A few of the viruses that can wreak havoc on your system include sin, pain, defeat and failure. When we don't renew our minds, they will ultimately lead us to our own personal blue screen of death. Hence, we end up going through the same cycles and habits of making bad decisions, repeating mistakes, following patterns of sin, and living in defeat. The reason we must be vigilant in renewing our minds is because our operating system is faulty. If we want to have the life God gave His son Jesus for us to have, we must renew our minds.

> "Do not be conformed to this world, but be transformed by the renewal of your mind, that by testing you may discern what is the will of God, what is good and acceptable and perfect." **Romans 12:2 (ESV)**

Our faulty minds cannot accurately and consistently discern what the good and acceptable perfect will of God is. **In order for us to know God's will and to apply it to our lives, we must renew our minds.** The primary way to renew your mind is to replace your current operating system with God's. Whereas your system was programmed by the world and flesh to embody selfishness and fear, which led to defeat and failure, God's operating system is His Word that leads to serving others, freedom from fear, and victory in Jesus.

Words are how we express thoughts. If you want to know what God thinks, read His Word! This is the primary way to renew your mind. When you meditate on God's Word, it transforms your mind. His truth replaces wrongful thinking. God's thoughts are perfect. Ours are flawed. God's thoughts lead to freedom, hope and victory as we live out His perfect will. Our thoughts lead to bondage, fear and defeat. Make no mistake, God's thoughts and ways are invariably greater than ours.

> "For my thoughts are not your thoughts,
> neither are your ways my ways,"
> declares the Lord.
> "As the heavens are higher than the earth,
> so are my ways higher than your ways
> and my thoughts than your thoughts.
> **Isaiah 55:8-9 (NIV)**

We renew our minds by reading the Bible, memorizing Scripture, and committing God's wisdom to memory. It is amazing to me that so many believers don't read their Bible. No wonder the statistics of the world regarding pornography, divorce, and other ungodly practices are also occurring in the church. The Bible contains life and power to change our thinking, and yet believers are often careless about reading it regularly. They would rather take someone else's word for it, and while it's good to listen to preachers and teachers of God's word, you won't be able to tell which ones are true and which ones are false without being grounded in the Word yourself.

> *My dear friends, don't believe everything you hear.*
> *Carefully weigh and examine what people tell you.*
> *Not everyone who talks about God comes from God.*
> *There are a lot of lying preachers loose in the world.*
> **1 John 4:1 (MSG)**

You cannot renew your mind without reading God's word. You cannot discern truth from lies without reading God's word. Fortunately, it's easier than ever to read the Bible today by using apps like YouVersion, study Bibles, etc. I cannot encourage you enough to get a Bible and establish a plan to read it daily. It will radically change your life, for the better!

> *Let the word of Christ richly dwell within you as you*
> *teach and admonish one another with all wisdom, and as*
> *you sing psalms, hymns, and spiritual songs with grati-*
> *tude in your hearts to God.* **Colossians 3:16 (ESV)**

Scripture Memorization

We also renew our minds by memorizing Scripture. Sometimes you can memorize scripture just by reading it. When you read God's Word you are downloading it into your mind and spirit. Other times, you will want to write a verse down, post it in a place you regularly visit (bathroom mirror, steering wheel, computer) and recite it aloud every time you see it until you have it committed to memory. I would encourage you to select verses to memorize that directly address areas of weakness, wrong thinking and fears. There are also a lot of apps that gamify scripture memorization and make it a fun endeavor through fill-in-the-blank puzzles, songs, word jumbles. Several of these apps even allow you to challenge friends and will track your progress in topics and various books of the Bible. You'll be amazed at how even a small effort consistently made will allow you to memorize a great deal of life-transforming scripture.

I have a friend whose wife became severely ill and developed amnesia. It was so bad, she didn't even recognize her husband or her own child. But there was one thing she could do. She could recite almost every scripture she had ever read. How is that possible? Because the Word of God is not only a mental book, it is spiritual. And it is living!

> *For the word of God is alive and powerful. It is sharper than the sharpest two-edged sword, cutting between soul and spirit, between joint and marrow. It exposes our innermost thoughts and desires.* **Hebrews 4:12 (NLT)**

Submitting to God's Word

Another way we renew our minds is by letting God's Word read us. Scripture says that God's word exposes our thoughts and desires. It brings to light what is really going on in our hearts. His truth not only sets us free from the bondage of sin, it reveals the lies we have believed, and guides us along the path to victory. However, it is of utmost importance that you settle in your heart that God's Word is the authority, not you. This means that you allow His Word to challenge and correct your thinking, not the other way around. Paul talks about how Christ makes the church clean by washing it with the water of

His Word. Immerse yourself in the Word and let it change you. Apply what the Bible says to your life and your relationships. Remember, it is cleansing and renewing your mind every time you read it.

> *He made the church holy by the power of his word,*
> *and he made it pure by washing it with water.*
> **Ephesians 5:26 (CEV)**

Confession

Our flesh is a strong opponent that prefers to fight one-on-one. It knows, as the enemy knows, that there is a greater chance of defeating you when you are all by yourself. One of the enemy's primary tactics to disrupt God's plan for our lives is isolation. When we are isolated and alone and have to fight one-on-one, we become vulnerable to being blindsided. We may also grow weary which causes us to overestimate our own ability. Isolation produces pride, defeat or a lethal combination of both in us as we attempt to fight the enemy.

The enemy prefers to fight in isolation because it is a dark place, and it is easier to deceive us in the dark. In the dark things seem larger, more serious, and more fearful because we cannot see clearly, or grasp the bigger picture. **Your flesh and sin thrive in isolation and secrecy.** Like mildew and mold, they grow stronger and more odious in dark places where it's easier to overpower you and direct your desires. **In stark contrast, freedom reigns in the light.** Therefore, we must emerge from the darkness of isolation and get into relationships with others in the light if we want to live in freedom.

> *Therefore, confess your sins to one another and pray for one another, that you may be healed. The prayer of a righteous person has great power as it is working.*
> **James 5:16 (ESV)**

Confession is a powerful weapon for crucifying our flesh and bringing healing and victory to our lives. In practical terms, confessing is simply letting someone else know what is happening in your mind, heart or body. When we keep something inside, it remains in the dark, but when we tell someone else, we bring it into the light where it can no longer thrive.

Victory in Jesus is never an individual feat, but the result of a unified team. Crucifying your flesh will take teamwork. James says we are to confess one to another. You cannot confess to yourself. We need relationships that are strong enough to handle our weaknesses and loving enough to protect us in those weaknesses. We need people we can trust who want to see us live spiritually victorious lives, not just successful lives. We need people we can call on at any time to confess our temptations and struggles, people who are willing to hold us accountable and help us to keep our flesh in check.

Accountability

There is no growth without accountability. You need to find someone you love and trust, who has a mature and growing relationship with Jesus, and who is willing to help you crucify your flesh by providing mutual accountability, prayer, and confession. *Please note*: social media is NOT a good partner for confession and accountability. A good partner is someone who loves you enough to hurt your feelings and heal your soul. Those friends are hard to come by, but when you find them, honor and keep them.

> *Faithful are the wounds of a friend;*
> *profuse are the kisses of an enemy.*
> **Proverbs 27:6 (ESV)**

Once you have built a relationship with a trusted friend, you need to set boundaries for one another. Both of you need to understand each other's areas of weakness so you can watch out for blind spots. For example, if you are weak in regard to lust, then it would be wise to use software like Covenant Eyes and give your friend access to all of your devices to help hold you accountable. If spiritual discipline is your weakness, then consider doing a Bible reading plan together. If finances are a weakness, keep your friend in the loop regarding your monthly budget and text them before you spend money on non-budgeted items. If you are weak in the area of sexual purity, ask your friend to help you set boundaries and give them access to your dating apps and messages.

Once you have set boundaries and expectations, you must also give your friend permission to regularly ask you hard questions. To have this discussion on the front end will provide a more natural relationship. There may come a time when you are struggling that you'll resent your friend for asking questions, but remember they are helping you stay the course and follow God's plan for a victorious life. Here are some questions you can ask each other to keep things in the light:

1. Have you been with a person in the past week in a way that could be viewed as compromising - either emotionally or physically?
2. Have all your financial dealings been performed with integrity?
3. Did your spending, saving and giving honor God?
4. Have you viewed any pornographic or sexually explicit material that would grieve the Holy Spirit?

5. Have you spent adequate time with Jesus in Bible study and prayer?
6. Have you spent quality time and given priority to your family?
7. Have you just lied to me about any of the above?

Remember accountability is highly desirable because it helps crucify our flesh so we can be led by God's desires for our lives. The enemy's tactic is to get you in isolation where he can lead you by the desires of your flesh. God's tactic is to get you into Gospel relationships where you'll be led by the desires of the Spirit. God wants to see your flesh defeated so your spirit can thrive, your mind renewed from your old way of thinking, and your blind spots protected by close friends who will love you enough to help you cover your weaknesses. God desires to see your sins exposed to the light of His love so the enemy is forced to surrender his power over you. Are you ready to crucify your flesh so that God can empower you with His Spirit?

9

Passion

The fire on the altar must be kept burning; it must not go out. Every morning the priest is to add firewood and arrange the burnt offering on the fire and burn the fat of the fellowship offerings on it. The fire must be kept burning on the altar continuously; it must not go out.
Leviticus 6:12-13 (NIV)

We are creatures of desire. **God's goal is not for us to be lifeless, but full of life.** Desire is the fuel for spiritual growth, and yet, we typically measure spiritual growth by knowledge and morality. While knowledge and morality are admirable and necessary qualities, they are terrible substitutes for desire and passion. In his book on desire, John Eldredge states, "The greatest enemy of holiness is not passion; it is apathy."[11] If we believe Eldredge's assertion that apathy kills more dreams and derails more destinies than passion, then we must continually seek to keep our passion for spiritual desires ignited so that we are not tempted by false desires or opportunities to fulfill our desires outside of God and His will.

Your godly desires and your fleshly desires are never lukewarm, stagnant or neutral. Desire is either hot or cold, growing or dying. I personally believe God ignites the fire of desire in our hearts, but it is our responsibility to keep the fire burning. So which desires are you currently fueling?

The thing about fires is that they naturally wane. In order to keep a fire burning you have to keep it stoked. You must daily place new fuel on the fire of your heart if it is to remain fiery. Many people neglect their spiritual fire soon after they are saved. Still others only tend their fire once a week at church, and even then they expect their pastor to stoke their fire for them. If you want to overcome the tactics of the enemy and live out your purpose, then you must check the fire of desire in your spirit each day. You must also invite the wind of the Holy Spirit to fan your spiritual flames into burning desires. And like the Israelites, you must gather fuel to burn, then vigilantly tend your fire.

Desires are the fuel that propel our direction in life. What we desire, we pursue. What we pursue shapes who we become. Who we become determines our destiny. In short, our desires are critical to our destiny. As preacher, Eric Thomas, says, "Where your focus goes, your energy flows." I cannot agree more, and would add, "What you focus on, you empower. What you empower, fuels your desires." When Paul is teaching the Galatians, he reveals to them that the best way to crucify flesh is to walk closely with God's Holy Spirit!

"But I say, walk by the Spirit, and you will not gratify the desires of the flesh."
Galatians 5:16 (ESV)

"If we live by the Spirit, let us also walk by the Spirit."
Galatians 5:25 NASB)

If we are being led by God's Spirit, then we cannot be led by our flesh. We can only be led by one person or thing at a time. We are called to be led by God's Spirit because God designed all of our desires and passions to be fulfilled by His Spirit. God wants us to live a full life of love, passion and fulfillment walking in His Spirit. Paul compares walking in the flesh and walking in the Spirit as two roots that produce two different fruits in our lives.

"For the desires of the flesh are against the Spirit, and the desires of the Spirit are against the flesh, for these are opposed to each other, to keep you from doing the things you want to do. But if you are led by the Spirit, you are not under the law. Now the works of the flesh are evident: sexual immorality, impurity, sensuality, idolatry, sorcery, enmity, strife, jealousy, fits of anger, rivalries, dissensions, divisions, envy, drunkenness, orgies, and things like these. I warn you, as I warned you before, that those who do such things will not inherit the kingdom of God. But the fruit of the Spirit is love, joy, peace, patience, kindness, goodness, faithfulness, gentleness, self-control; against such things there is no law."

Galatians 5:17-23 (ESV)

We walk in the flesh when we allow our flesh to be the guiding authority of the decisions we make. Unfortunately, when we live by our flesh it produces fruit (consequences) that we have to live with. We walk in the Spirit by allowing God's Holy Spirit to work in us and through us. We crucify the flesh, but yield to the Spirit.

But the Helper, the Holy Spirit, whom the Father will send in My name, He will teach you all things, and bring to your remembrance all that I said to you.

John 14:26 (ESV)

Our Helper

Jesus calls the Holy Spirit our helper. He wants to help us live the full life Jesus died for us to have. He wants to help us know our identity in Christ and God's will for our lives. He wants to help us grow into maturity and discern God's truth over the enemy's lies. He wants to help us overcome sin and temptation. He wants to help us reach our destiny and receive the Crown of Life from Jesus. The Holy Spirit is our helper, not our doer. He helps by coming alongside of us and encouraging and equipping us to do God's will. He is unlimited in power and ability, but He is a Spirit, which is where we, as the body of Christ, come in. On this earth, we are the hands, feet and voice of Jesus, and the Holy Spirit helps us to do His work of loving our neighbors and fulfilling the Great Commission. You are an important member of the body of Christ and you are needed by the Holy Spirit to be His physical expression of God's grace, love and mercy here on earth. If we want to reach our destiny, then we must be willing to yield to His influence. We must get to know God's Spirit and His ways intimately. How do we do this? Through His Word, worship and prayer.

Be Filled

How can we be led by the Spirit, walk by the Spirit, and live lives empowered by the Spirit? First, we must grow in our awareness of the Spirit's reality and presence in our lives. Then, we must submit our desires and will to Him. Finally, we must die to ourselves and invite the Holy Spirit of God to fill us.

> *And do not get drunk with wine, for that is debauchery,*
> *but be filled with the Spirit, addressing one another in*
> *psalms and hymns and spiritual songs, singing*
> *and making melody to the Lord with your heart,*
> *giving thanks always and for everything to God*
> *the Father in the name of our Lord Jesus Christ,*

submitting to one another out of reverence for Christ.
Ephesians 5:18-21 (ESV)

Paul's words to us are not a recommendation, but a command. He wants us to understand the importance of being filled by the Spirit and how critical it is to our daily spiritual victory. I cannot emphasize enough how essential the Holy Spirit's power is to the fulfilling of your purpose and plans for your life. In his blog post on Ephesians 5:18, pastor Ray Pritchard wrote:

> *The filling of the Spirit is the most important doctrine of the spiritual life. It is foundational to everything else. There is nothing we need more. Here is my definition of the filling of the Spirit: It is that state in which the Holy Spirit is free to do all He came into my life to do. In a sense being filled with the Spirit is an impossibility-at least as far as it depends on us. Only God's Spirit can fill us. We need two things-emptiness and openness. You can't fill a jar that's already full, and you can't fill a jar that is not open. There must be a sense of need-"Lord, I'm empty and I need to be filled by Your Spirit." There must be a willingness- "Lord, I'm open to You..." The filling of the Spirit is really as simple as that. As long as we are conscious of our need and as long as we are willing to yield to the Lord, we can be filled with the Lord all day long. This power is available to us all day long.*[12]

To be filled with the Spirit is to be aware and open to His movement in your life. To the extent that you make room for Him in your life is the extent to which He will fill you. This means emptying yourself of sin, human will, fleshly desires and your own power, and being open to Him pouring His will, His desires and His power into you.

Being filled with the Spirit is a daily tactic for you to walk in spiritual victory and power over sin and the flesh. The disciples received the Holy Spirit when Jesus revealed Himself to them after His resurrection, and breathed upon them.

> *On the evening of that day, the first day of the week, the doors being locked where the disciples were for fear of the Jews, Jesus came and stood among them and said to them, Peace be with you. When he had said this, he showed them his hands and his side. Then the disciples were glad when they saw the Lord. Jesus said to them again, Peace be with you. As the Father has sent me, even so I am sending you. And when he had said this, he breathed on them and said to them, Receive the Holy Spirit.*
> **John 20:19-22 (ESV)**

This scenario takes place after Jesus paid the price for all sin, purchasing salvation for mankind by becoming the perfect holy sacrifice for us upon the cross. Jesus had also spent three days in the grave taking the keys to death, hell and the grave from Satan (Revelation 1:18), and preaching the gospel to the people who died before Him (1 Peter 3:18-20). Jesus rose from the grave to show us that He has the power of life and wants to freely give it to all who accept Him as Lord and Savior. The disciples had heard the gospel from Jesus and believed, and now they received the power of the Holy Spirit to live out the good news of the gospel in their lives and share it with others.

When Jesus breathed upon them, He released His Spirit to live within them. The same breath that He exhaled into Adam in order to bring him to life (Genesis 2:7) Jesus now breathed into His freshly born- again disciples. At this moment, we can say that they received the Holy Spirit, or had the Holy Spirit.

The encounter described in John 20:19 between the resurrected Jesus and the disciples was His first meeting with them since the Last Supper. There is some biblical evidence presented by Bible historians who believe that this encounter took place on April 9th, or Nisan 19 in the Jewish calendar. If we fast-forward to May 18, or Iyar 27 in the Jewish calendar, which is about 40 days after Jesus breathed upon His disciples and they received the Holy Spirit, He gives them some instructions before He ascends back to His throne to sit at the right hand of the Father.

> *"And while staying with them he ordered them not to depart from Jerusalem, but to wait for the promise of the Father, which, he said, you heard from me; for John baptized with water, but you will be baptized with the Holy Spirit not many days from now. So when they had come together, they asked him, Lord, will you at this time restore the kingdom to Israel? He said to them, It is not for you to know times or seasons that the Father has fixed by his own authority. But you will receive power when the Holy Spirit has come upon you, and you will be my witnesses in Jerusalem and in all Judea and Samaria, and to the end of the earth. And when he had said these things, as they were looking on, he was lifted up, and a cloud took him out of their sight."* **Acts 1:4-9 (ESV)**

Wait? Why would Jesus tell His disciples to wait for the Holy Spirit to baptize them if they had already received the Holy Spirit? Didn't they already have the Holy Spirit? If so, what in the world are they waiting for? Well, we know that what Jesus promised them would come with power that they did not have yet, but would need in order to live the life that God had planned for them. It was important enough that Jesus didn't want them to go preach the gospel, or heal the sick or share His love with anyone — yet. It was important enough that Jesus pushed the pause button on the Great Commission. Let that sink in a moment. This power that Jesus promised the disciples was important enough that He didn't want to build His church or advance His mission until they received it.

The disciples obeyed Jesus and waited for what He promised. Think about that. Not just the fact that they instantly obeyed Him, but the patience they manifested by doing so... and for ten long days! And the reward was tremendous. I don't know about you, but I don't like to wait. Could you imagine you and your church locking yourselves up in a room for 10 days without killing each other? Nevertheless, their patience and unity was rewarded on the tenth day when Jesus, faithful to His promise, poured out the power of His Spirit upon them.

> *When the day of Pentecost arrived, they were all together in one place. And suddenly there came from heaven a sound like a mighty rushing wind, and it filled the entire house where they were sitting. And divided tongues as of fire appeared to them and rested on each one of them. And they were all filled with the Holy Spirit and began to speak in other tongues as the Spirit gave them utterance.*
> **Acts 2:1-4 (ESV)**

At this moment, God pushed the button to launch His church, His mission, and the purpose for each of the individual disciples. What was the catalyst? Being filled with the Spirit of God! Do you believe you and I are any different? Do you believe that we need the same thing, if not more of what the disciples had? They walked with Jesus in the flesh and still needed His Spirit to do what God had called them to do. God's primary tactic for you then, is to live out His purpose through obedience to the Holy Spirit in your life, your church and your family, that all may be filled with His Spirit. Yes, you received His Spirit the moment you were saved, just like the disciples received the Holy Spirit when Jesus breathed upon them. But have you been filled with His Spirit and the Spirit's power?

What's the difference between receiving the Spirit and being filled with the Spirit? You receive the Spirit through Jesus' work and salvation in your life. You are filled with the Spirit as you become aware of the Spirit of God inside of you and allow Him to fill you from the inside out. I personally believe that those 10 days in the upper room were extremely important. I believe it was during those 10 days that the disciples were in prayer, worshiping Jesus, and focused on His glory, beauty and power, that they were awakened to the reality that the Spirit of Jesus was living on the inside of them. The same Spirit that resurrected Jesus was alive inside of them (Romans 8:11)! I believe they were awakened to the reality that just like the Spirit of God worked from the inside of the tomb to the outside, the Holy Spirit was working on the inside of them and wanted to be manifested through them to the outside world.

If you want to be filled with the Holy Spirit, you simply submit to Him and open yourself to the Spirit's move in your life. **The Holy Spirit is a gentleman and He will not impose Himself upon anyone. He only comes when invited through faith. He is also not pushy. He will not try to fill anyone who is already full of themselves.** If He did try to fill us when we are full of ourselves, it would cause a mess. Therefore, He only fills us to the extent that we empty ourselves. Find your own Upper Room, where you can empty yourself of your desires and your will and submit to the Spirit in prayer and worship. Pray that the Spirit who lives on the inside of you would fill every part of you. Give Him permission to fill your heart, mind, soul and body with His love, His power and His ways. Then, be in awe of what He does in you and through you!

What is holding you back from allowing God to fill you with His Spirit? Is it tradition? Is it fear? Is it comfort? Is it pride? Is it lack of understanding? Being filled by God's Spirit does not make you a better Christian. It simply makes you a more powerful one! For you to defeat the enemy's tactics you will need all the power you can get. You definitely cannot do it on your own power. The only way you will overcome his tactics is through the power of the Spirit. Are you trying to live your Christian life based on your own power or through the power of the Holy Spirit? Have you had your own personal Upper Room experience where you were filled by the Holy Spirit? If not, read the book of Acts and ask yourself if you are living New Testament Christianity or American denominational Christianity. Then, seek God and ask Him in faith to fill you with everything He has for you!

10

Deception

*But I am afraid that as the serpent deceived Eve by his cunning, your
thoughts will be led astray from a sincere and pure devotion to Christ.*
2 Corinthians 11:3 (ESV)

Full of excitement, John left work on a Friday and headed home to
pack his bag and load up the SUV. It had been a long week of meetings,
sales calls and mandatory reports, but tomorrow was the day he and his
son were going on a fishing trip to the San Juan River in the western
United States. He could not wait to spend time with his son and teach
him the ins and outs of fly fishing like his father had taught him. He had
fallen in love with fly fishing on a weekend fishing trip with his dad who
had bought him his first rod and reel for his 10th birthday. Now John
planned to give this same rod and reel to his son on their trip.

John's dad taught him how to fly cast with precision and land a good
spot on the top of the water. It took a lot of practice and tangled up line,
but he now tells people he's the best fly caster east of the Mississippi. His
dad also taught him the art of tying his own flies using a variety of different knots to ensure the fly and the hook remained intact throughout
the rigors of casting. His dad taught him to analyze the environment he
fished, carefully observing the various types of trees, grass and shrubs
thriving by the river. He taught him to sit down and watch the river before fishing, taking in its function and flow and paying special attention
to the different kinds of bugs, flies and insects that dwelt in the area and
landed on the water's surface.

John believed observing the river was the secret to great fly fishing and he wanted to teach his son how to do it well during their trip. Most fishermen buy the latest gear and hope the fish will bite the artificial flies they bought at a tackle store. John knew that the best way to catch a beautiful Rainbow Trout was to fish with a fly that matched what the fish was already eating. Therefore, he would spend time observing the river and then he would tie a fly from natural material he found along the river. This gave the fly a familiar color, look and smell that would entice the fish to feel comfortable taking the bait.

As John and his son approached the river that Saturday morning, his son ran toward the water excited to catch his first Rainbow. John told him before they fished, they needed to sit back and observe the environment. He showed him a bright colored insect that flew right by their heads and landed on the water. They observed that the insect was blue-green in color with feathery wings. John told his son that if that bug is what's landing on the water, then that bug is what the monster Rainbows were used to eating and wanted to eat.

John and his son started looking around the river for items they could use to simulate the bright colored insect they saw land on the river. John found a shrub with a feathery stalk. His son found a flower with the same blue-green color of the insect. They brought their findings together and John showed his son how to camouflage the hook by folding the feathery stalk around it and making it look like insect wings. Then, he took the flower bloom and wrapped it around the middle part of the stalk to mimic the body of the insect. John's son could not believe how much the fly they had just made looked like the insect they had observed.

Next, John showed his son how to cast a couple of times and then let him cast himself. After about five casts he had figured it out. John pointed him in a direction where the fish would naturally be in the afternoon, and told him to cast there. He showed him how to hesitate and slowly flicker the fly once he had cast it on the water. He explained that flies don't land and then fly away, they land, move a little bit, and then fly away.

His son tried the hesitation technique with the custom fly they had made a couple of times when suddenly, he had a bite. He began reeling the fish in and as it got closer he could see it was big beautiful Rainbow Trout. It was a memorable moment that neither of them would ever forget. Unfortunately for the fish, it was its last memory!

John knew what the fish wanted. More importantly, he knew exactly what the fish in that specific river wanted, and he gave it to them. Well, technically the fish didn't get what it wanted, although the fly looked, smelled, and acted like what the fish wanted. However, hidden inside what appeared to be a perfect opportunity was a hook that would hold onto the fish once it chose to pursue its desire. Looks can be deceiving.

No fisherman would ever go fishing with just a hook, and no Rainbow Trout would ever go after a line with just a hook on it. Why? Because fish are not attracted to a hook. They are attracted to what they desire. Fishermen have to deceive the fish into taking the hook by hiding it inside everything the fish wants and desires.

The enemy knows we would never consciously pursue disobedience and death. No one wakes up and says, "Today seems like a good day to have an affair!" Or, "I feel like getting a DUI, today!"
Or, "I've marked my calendar to get addicted to drugs and pornography today." The enemy knows that we would not choose spiritual death or even long-lasting negative consequences. The only way he can tempt us to choose death is to deceive us into biting a death hook camouflaged by our desires.

> "All is clouded by desire: as fire by smoke, as a mirror by dust. Through these it blinds the soul."
> ~ **C.J. Koch, _The Year Of Living Dangerously_**

The enemy has been fishing for a long, long time. He started in the

Garden of Eden and has never taken a break. He has become a pro observing the environment, the history and the desires of each person he seeks to tempt away from God's promises and love. He knows what sins you really enjoyed before you gave your life to Jesus. He knows what parts of your flesh you have not completely crucified. He knows what desires you have that you want fulfilled more than anything in the world. He pays attention. He observes. Then, he creates a hook camouflaged by everything you have ever wanted and he casts it right in front of your face at just the right time. He is a really good fisher of men and women. A quick history lesson of great men and women of God who have fallen into sin and disgrace will show you just how masterful he is at deception.

> "When he [Satan] lies, he speaks his native language,
> for he is a liar and the father of lies."
> **John 8:44 (NIV)**

One of the most famous men of God who took the enemy's bait was Jimmy Swaggart. He was one of the most recognizable, influential ministers in the world in the '70s and '80s until his adulterous affair with a prostitute. His ministry flourished under a great spotlight and gave him the resources to send millions of dollars all over the world to support orphanages, schools, missions organizations and more. The enemy didn't want this to continue, so he carefully observed Jimmy's environment, history and desires. He began to slowly cast Jimmy's unmet desires in front of him. It probably began with the enemy casting an attractive woman in Jimmy's path who gave him the kind of attention he found hard to ignore and sent his imagination soaring.

As the enemy continued to desensitize Jimmy's thoughts, he upped the ante with each cast. Before long, Jimmy was deceived into believing he could have his desires fulfilled and still serve God . The enemy had him. He finally cast the big hook wrapped up in lust, unfulfilled desires, power, secrecy and intimacy. Jimmy couldn't see the hook that was tied to disgrace, shame, embarrassment, guilt and a great fall from influence. He couldn't see the hook, so he took a big bite and was snagged.

Many of us, myself included, have looked at Jimmy with judgmental eyes without considering how we, too, could find ourselves in a similar situation, maybe not as public, but devastating all the same. The enemy is skillful in using our desires against us. **He does not take on the appearance of evil when he comes to tempt us. He comes to us looking like an angel of light.** I think one of his great deceptions is using horror movies to make himself look evil and grotesque. We view him as this fictitious monster that is easily spotted due to his horns, dark appearance and creepy voice. Most of us have not encountered that guy, but we have encountered an angel of light that has offered us everything we have ever wanted and desired, while appearing kind, soft-spoken and gentle. He is really good at deception.

> But I am not surprised! Even Satan disguises himself as an angel of light.
> **2 Corinthians 11:14 (NLT)**

The enemy comes into our lives as an angel of light. He is immensely beautiful on the outside but corrupt on the inside. He is a Trojan horse. Like the Greeks used as a gift filled with death to invade the city of Troy, the enemy will infiltrate your life by offering gifts that are filled with death and the enemy's devices to defeat you.

On April 24, 1184 BCE, the city of Troy fell to invading Greek armies, ending the Trojan War. The Trojan War is an important story in Greek mythology and literature. The ancient Greek poet Homer wrote about the final days of the Trojan War in his epic work, The Iliad.

The Trojan War began when a Trojan prince ran off with the wife of a Greek king. The woman, Helen of Troy, became "the face that launched a thousand ships," when her husband, Menelaus, assembled a fleet of ships to retrieve her from Troy. The war between the Greeks (who actually called themselves Achaeans) and the Trojans lasted ten years.

The Trojan War ended when the Greek commander Odysseus devised a plan to invade the walled city. The Greeks pretended to give up. Before leaving the Trojan beaches, they gave the Trojans a present—a giant wooden horse. The Trojans opened the gates to accept the horse. Inside the hollow horse were armed Greek troops, who sacked the city.[13]

Satan is a Trojan Horse that seeks to enter your life through whatever you desire and whatever you believe you need at the time. The fact that Satan comes as an angel of light should illustrate how deceptive and conniving he is. He is as dark, grotesque, and evil as anything that has ever existed, yet he appears to us as a beautiful helper in our time of need. He comes to us as a compassionate friend in a time of loneliness. He comes to us as an understanding soul when our spouse doesn't understand us. He comes to us as the opportunity we've been hoping, dreaming and praying for. He comes to us as everything we could ever want. He has camouflaged his evil in light.

This truth means we have to be attentive to what we are drawn to. We have to be careful of what we want. As Rumi said, "Be suspicious of what you want." The writer of Proverbs gives us this insight, "Desire without knowledge is not good, and whoever makes haste with his feet misses his way (Proverbs 19:2)." You have to test what you want through God's Word and through God's plan and purpose for you. Remember that the Trojan Horse was a gift that the Spartans wanted! They fully received the gift because they wanted it. Be very careful and very suspicious of gifts! Many times they come with strings attached.

The enemy does not want to fight you from the outside in. No, he knows he cannot win that way. He knows that you are well equipped with the armor of God and the power of God's Spirit. In order for his tactics to be successful, he has to fight you from the inside out. He wants to defeat you by getting into your life, your thoughts and your heart through open doors and by invitation. He will either use a Trojan Horse or possibly send in a Fifth Column.

The Fifth Column

A couple of years ago I read an incredible book by Dag Mills titled, "Loyalty & Disloyalty" where the author shares a story about an army general who surrounded a large city with the aim of conquering it. The city was heavily fortified with a high and imposing gate. The army general surrounded the city in readiness to attack.

One friend of the general came along and asked him, "Sir, how do you think you are going to overcome the defense of this fortified city? No one in recent history has been able to conquer this great city?"

The army general smiled and said, "It's my fifth column. I'm depending on them to do the trick."

The general's friend was very interested and asked, "What is the fifth column? I thought you only had four columns?"

The army general replied, "I do have a fifth column."

"Oh, I see. Is it a special commando unit or are they airborne troopers?" the man asked.

The general laughed, "No, it's none of these. My fifth column consists of my spies, agents, friends, and supporters who are already within the city. You just wait. They will open those big gates from within and my armies will rush in."[14]

The enemy's tactics are to deceive you into letting small deceptions into your life so that they open the big gates of your heart to allow the enemy to rush in like a flood (Isaiah 59:19). Even Solomon, the wisest man who ever lived, said it's the small foxes that spoil the vine (Song of Solomon 2:15). Don't let the enemy deceive with little sins and compromises because those small foxes will spoil the fruitfulness of your vine and infiltrate your life like a fifth column looking to open the gates of your heart to the enemy and his attacks.

11

Patience

And thus Abram, having patiently waited, obtained the promise.
Hebrews 6:15 (ESV)

The enemy knows we are not patient people. He knows we want all of God's promises and blessings — Right Now! Far be it from us to wait a minute longer than we have to. And while we know God is always on time, if we were honest, we'd much rather He was on our time. That you secretly believe your timing is better than God's might be hard to admit, but we're all guilty of speculation, given the right circumstances. So... consider this your first I.A. Meeting. What is I.A.? Impatience Anonymous! The enemy knows we desire God's timing to be our timing, so his most frequent tactic where we're concerned is delay.

God's promises are incredible. Because they are such wonderful promises, we find it difficult to wait on them. It's like being a kid and having to wait until Christmas to open the beautifully wrapped packages under the tree. You pick up the gifts to see how much they weigh and shake them to guess the contents. Why? Because you know there is something in the package that will bring joy and happiness to your life and you cannot wait to experience it.

When I was around 10 years old, all I wanted for Christmas was a pair of Michael Jordan basketball shoes. All of my friends at school had "Jordans", which made me want them even more. The problem was that our family didn't have a lot of extra money for expensive basketball shoes. That fact didn't faze me, though. I told my parents over and over that was all I wanted for Christmas.

I was hoping and expecting to get Jordans for Christmas and I couldn't wait for the 25th to arrive. I started looking through all the hiding places my parents had for gifts. Then, one glorious day I climbed to the top of their closet and found two shoe boxes. I could hardly contain my excitement.

When Christmas Eve came, I couldn't sleep. The next morning my brother and I woke my parents bright and early so we could start opening gifts. I immediately grabbed the shoebox-sized gift and ripped through the wrapping paper to find that my shoes were Jordache, not Jordans! My mind raced. "How could this happen? Do my parents even love me? Is this a cruel joke?" I wanted, no I needed, Jordans not Jordache!

Then, I watched my little brother unwrap a shoebox-sized gift. I thought to myself, "If my parents got my little brother my Jordans, I will destroy him!" As he removed the wrapping paper the shoebox came into full focus. He had MJs, but something was wrong. They didn't look like the Jordan's the other kids at school were wearing. I moved in closer to "congratulate" my brother on his gift, and saw that the shoes were indeed MJs, but not Michael Jordans. They were British Knights' Michael Jackson shoes. What a cruel world!

That year, I couldn't wait for the gift to come so I tried to make it happen on my own by campaigning for it from my parents and attempting to find it early. Sadly, I did not get Jordans that Christmas or on my 11th birthday. In fact, it took me a couple of years to work and save up my money to buy my own. I did not get them on my timing. My timing was delayed.

Delayed promises are great tests of our faith and one specific area in which the enemy succeeds in his efforts to tempt us out of God's promises and plans. You see the enemy loves to tempt us during any delay between God's promise and the fulfillment of that promise. The waiting is where we are tempted and deceived. He fills the gap between promise and fulfillment with confusion that makes us wonder if the promise was truly for us. Will it actually happen? Has God forgotten about us? These questions leave us trying to figure out God's ways and plans for ourselves. Unfortunately we often come to the conclusion that we need to make it happen on our own.

Abram, who would later be named Abram, had a very unique relationship with God. God specifically selected him to be a founding father of His people on earth. Abram did nothing to earn this privilege. God simply chose him. When God selected Abram, He also gave Him a great promise. In Genesis 12:2-3, God tells Abram, *"And I will make of you a great nation, and I will bless you and make your name great, so that you will be a blessing. I will bless those who bless you, and him who dishonors you I will curse, and in you all the families of the earth shall be blessed."*

He promises Abram land, people, and His blessing. God even goes into more detail to describe the promise to Abram by having him look at the sand upon the beach. He tells Abram his descendants will be more in number than all the grains of sand he can see on the beach. Then, God makes the promise even more vivid. He tells Abram to look at the stars. Abram lifts his head and sees a pitch black sky illuminated by vast sums of sparkling stars as far as the eye can see. Genesis 15:5 describes it this way:

> *"And he brought him outside and said, Look toward heaven, and number the stars, if you are able to number them. Then he said to him, So shall your offspring be."*

Wow! What a sight. What a promise!

Abram was obviously excited about this promise. He was going to have children, and a whole lot of them. The Duggar's weren't going to have anything on Abram! If I'd been Abram I would have thought that in order for this promise to be fulfilled, I would need to get busy making babies! After all, Abram wasn't a young man. Most theologians believe he was around 75-years-old when God called him to follow Him and gave him the promise. Sure, 75 may be the new 65, but simple math tells us it is going to be difficult to have a couple billion babies when you start at 75 years of age.

Abram believed God's promise, but now he was in the delay game. He had received the promise, but it had yet to be fulfilled. It is during such delay that the enemy goes to work to get us off track, fill us with doubt and tempt us away from God's plan and presence. The enemy will always try to work in the area of delay, so imagine what Abram was going through.

On his 76th birthday, he still had no child with Sarai.
On his 77th birthday, he still had no child with Sarai.
On his 78th birthday, he still had no child with Sarai.
On his 79th birthday, he still had no child with Sarai.
On his 80th birthday, he still had no child with Sarai.
On his 81st birthday, he still had no child with Sarai.
On his 82nd birthday, he still had no child with Sarai.
On his 83rd birthday, he still had no child with Sarai.
On his 84th birthday, he still had no child with Sarai.
On his 85th birthday, he still had no child with Sarai.

As you can see, Abram was not getting younger. Each year he had to face the reality of what appeared to be a delay in God's promise to him. Maybe you are facing delay as well. Maybe God promised you a child and you have yet to get pregnant. Maybe God called you to ministry, but you have not yet seen that come to pass. Maybe God promised you that you would be healed of a disease, pain or sickness, but you are still dealing with it. Maybe God promised you a spouse, and yet you are still single and waiting. Maybe God promised you that a friend or family member would get saved, but they are still far away from the Lord. Maybe you could list your birthdays and write out next to it the promise that you are waiting on as well.

It is in delay that the enemy gets to even the greatest men and women of faith. Abram was a man of faith, so much so that God planned to build His family through him. The enemy began tempting Abram and deceiving him through the delay of God's promise. As Abram saw more birthdays come and go and the promise of God still not fulfilled, the enemy began deceiving Abram and Sarai into thinking it was their job to fulfill God's promise. The enemy made them believe they could have God's promises by taking control and making it happen by themselves.

"Now Sarai, Abram's wife, had borne him no children. She had a female Egyptian servant whose name was Hagar. And Sarai said to Abram, Behold now, the Lord has prevented me from bearing children. Go in to my servant; it may be that I shall obtain children by her. And Abram listened to the voice of Sarai. So, after Abram had lived ten years in the land of Canaan, Sarai, Abram's wife, took Hagar the Egyptian, her servant, and gave her to Abram her husband as a wife. And he went in to Hagar, and she conceived. And when she saw that she had conceived, she looked with contempt on her mistress." **Genesis 16:1-4**

Sarai was more focused on God's promise being fulfilled than she was on God, His ability and His faithfulness. The enemy had convinced her that God had prevented her from bearing a child. Wow! The delay game is a powerful tactic. **The enemy will use our delay to cause us to blame God for His promise not being fulfilled**. He had deceived her into questioning God's faithfulness. This is common during the delay game because we get so fixated on the promise of God that in our minds anything and anyone who doesn't serve the purpose becomes the cause of our promise not being fulfilled.

Quick question, have you started blaming God as the cause for your promise not being fulfilled? Have you started questioning His faithfulness?

When we begin to question God's faithfulness and ability, we place our trust in our own faithfulness and ability, which usurps God's will for our lives. Sarai placed her trust in her own plans more than in God's. She trusted her faithfulness to God's promise more than God's faithfulness to His own promise. Taking matters into her own hands, she quit walking by faith, justifying her plans by focusing on what she expected to accomplish. Often when we take matters into our own hands we justify our actions because when things go south, as they always do, we refuse to take the responsibility. Instead, we point the finger at God because we've decided if He loved us and cared for us, we'd already have what we wanted. Sarai rationalizes that since God has delayed His promise and prevented her from conceiving, she can pick up where He left off and fix the problems God caused in her and Abram's lives.

Sarai tells Abram to take her servant, Hagar, and get started making babies. This is marriage suicide, so guys, don't get any dumb ideas. Abram is being set up to be the villain in a dramatic BC episode equivalent to a Jerry Springer paternity show. If Hagar doesn't get pregnant, then Sarai is going to blame Abram for the lack of the promise being fulfilled. If Hagar does get pregnant, then Sarai has to suffer the pain of seeing her promise fulfilled by someone else. I promise you that one of the most difficult things anyone would ever have to deal with is seeing your promise, blessing or dreams fulfilled through someone else.

Sarai convinced Abram to fulfill God's promise her way. Think about that. The Bible describes Abram as a man of faith and promise, a man who left everything behind to obey God's command. And now, this man who trusted God with his entire life is not trusting God to do what He said He would do. Why would Abram go from complete trust in God to doubting God's ability? Because "his" promise was delayed, and it seemed it would never come to pass. That is how the enemy accomplishes his mission, by creating havoc during the delay between our promise and its fulfillment.

While we are waiting on our promise, God is working on His plan to fulfill it. God is not slow, He is steady. Even though you don't see any progress in the fulfilling of your promise, it does not mean God is not working on it behind the scenes. If you could see behind the scenes of your life, you would see God guiding you and bringing the right people into your life to help you along your path. You would see Him removing people the enemy sends your way to get you off track. You would see Him guiding you through different experiences that ultimately build character, integrity and faith, and you would learn to recognize God's efforts on your behalf and realize His promise will come to fulfillment in your lifetime. God is working!

Abram forgot that the promise was God's, not his. Since it *was* God's promise, then it was only God who was capable of fulfilling it. All Abram had to do was trust in God. The 16 years of delay gave the enemy the perfect opportunity to deceive Abram into thinking it was his promise and that he needed to trust himself instead of God. Abram learned a very costly lesson. Whenever we trust in ourselves more than in God, there is always a price to pay.

Although Abram received a son, Ishmael, he was not the son of promise since Ishmael was not Abram and Sarai's son. Ishmael was the son of Abram's effort to speed up the promises God had made him. God wanted Abram to experience the promise through God's ability, not through Abram's inability. God wanted the promise to be an illustration of His grace and power for the world to see. Ishmael was the fruit of Abram's efforts, ability and works. God did not want to build His family through the efforts of men. He wanted to build His family through grace.

Grace is the difference between our ability and God's promises. When we reach our limitations, grace makes up the difference. When we can't keep God's holy laws, grace makes up the difference. When we don't have the ability to fulfill God's purpose or calling, grace makes up the difference.

The enemy likes to fill the gap between our ability and God's promise with effort and works. He wants to bring the focus and attention back to us. He deceives us into working out our own plan to make God's promises come to fulfillment in our lives. The Bible is full of examples: from Abram trying to force God's promise of a family to fruition by having a child with a slave, or King Saul acting as his own priest and abandoning God's promise to give him direction on how to win the battle he faced (1 Samuel 13:8-9), to our own foolish attempts to "earn" God's promised _gift_ of salvation through works instead of trusting in His grace. The enemy wants you to doubt God and His ability and instead put your faith in yourself. Why? Because it's the fast-track to failure.

> _Thus says the Lord: "Cursed is the man who trusts in man and makes flesh his strength, whose heart turns away from the Lord._ **Jeremiah 17:5 (ESV)**

If we focus on ourselves and our abilities, we will fail and never see God's plan fulfilled in our lives. The enemy knows this because he has lived it. He knows the fruit of trying to do things his own way. He attempted to do things his own way and lost his position and place in heaven and is now eternally separated from God. What's worse is that he wants us to join him in his misery. He knows that if you keep your attention on God and His ability, there are no limitations to what God can do in and through you!

> *Jesus looked at them and said,*
> *"With man this is impossible, but*
> *with God all things are possible."*
> **Matthew 19:26 (NIV)**

Are you waiting on God's promise to be fulfilled in your life? Have you experienced the enemy trying to deceive you into making it happen your own way? Have you considered a strategy to expedite the promise? Are you focused on your ability and timing instead of trusting in God? If you answered yes to any of these questions, you are in the middle of the delay game, but I want to encourage you to wait for the Son of the Promise and don't try to fulfill God's promise through your own efforts. God's way is less costly and more rewarding than your way, so be patient. If God made the promise, you can count on His faithfulness. He cannot lie and His word will not return to Him void.

"For my thoughts are not your thoughts, neither are your
ways my ways," declares the Lord. "As the heavens are
higher than the earth, so are my ways higher than your
ways and my thoughts than your thoughts. As the rain
and the snow come down from heaven, and do not return

to it without watering the earth and making it bud and
flourish, so that it yields seed for the sower and bread for
the eater, so is my word that goes out from my mouth: It
will not return to me empty, but will accomplish what I
desire and achieve the purpose for which I sent it."
Isaiah 55:8-11 (NIV)

Delayed Consequences

While some of us are aware we are in a period of delay while waiting on God to fulfill His promises in our lives, others are experiencing delay and may not even realize it. That's because God has delayed the consequences of their decisions or actions. Delayed consequences occur when we have made a decision that should result in a negative outcome, but those consequences have not yet been fulfilled. In other words, you've been doing something you shouldn't, but you haven't been caught — yet. Or, you've been doing something unhealthy and haven't seen the fruit of it — yet. For example, if you eat greasy hamburgers all the time, but you haven't experienced negative health effects, the consequences of your actions are delayed.

The enemy's tactic when we experience delayed consequences is to tempt us to take God's grace and mercy for granted. Sometimes we engage in habitual sin and ignore our need to repent or confess to God because we haven't experienced the consequences of our sin. Perhaps we haven't felt shame because our sin is still a secret. Maybe we suppressed feelings of guilt by justifying our actions in our own eyes we could be toying with the idea of staying in sin a little longer by telling ourselves that God loves us and is a forgiving God. Of course this is true, but He is also a God of justice and truth. We must not deceive ourselves. All sin not covered in the blood of Jesus will reap negative consequences, and sin is not covered until we confess it and turn from it. In his letter to the Romans, Paul makes it abundantly clear that habitual sin leads to death and habitual obedience leads to righteousness.

What then? Are we to sin because we are not under the law but under grace? By no means! Do you not know that if you present yourselves to anyone as obedient slaves, you are slaves of the one whom you obey, either of sin, which leads to death, or of obedience, which leads to righteousness?
Romans 6:15-16 (ESV)

Yes, God is gracious and patient, but don't let the enemy use a delay in consequences to lull you into a life of sin and disobedience. As creatures who respond to rewards and consequences, it can be tempting to think that a behavior is okay or not as bad as people say it is when consequences are delayed. In Genesis 3, the enemy used delayed consequences to deceive Adam and Eve into disobeying God.

"You will not certainly die," the serpent said to the woman. "For God knows that when you eat from it your eyes will be opened, and you will be like God, knowing good and evil.
Genesis 3:1-5 (NIV)

Eve knew what the consequences were. She knew that if she ate of the tree that she would die. The serpent, who was crafty, used delayed consequences to trick her into disobeying God and disrupting God's plan. She ate the fruit of the tree but did she die? Well, not right away. The consequences of her action were delayed. It is only by God's grace that the consequences of our actions are delayed. If not for His grace, planet earth would be empty! The Apostle Peter says it this way:

> *"The Lord is not slow to fulfill his promise as some count slowness, but is patient toward you, not wishing that any should perish, but that all should reach repentance."*
> **2 Peter 3:9 (ESV)**

God is patiently delaying the consequences of our actions hoping that we will repent before the consequences are fulfilled.

The enemy uses God's grace to deceive us into abusing God's mercy and patience. When we don't experience immediate consequences, we can fall into the temptation to keep doing things our own way. Solomon explained that the reason people sin is because consequences are delayed.

> *"Because the sentence against an evil deed is not executed speedily, the heart of the children of man is fully set to do evil."*
> **Ecclesiastes 8:11 (ESV)**

I personally believe that if God did not delay the consequences of our sin, most of us would be more vigilant in our efforts to refrain from sinning - or we would be dead because we had sinned. Could you imagine being in a store where people were shoplifting and instead of security guards chasing them down, God opened up the ground and the shoplifters fell into a deep crevice directly into the pits of hell? I don't think anyone else in the store would be tempted to shoplift!

Julie Ackerman shares similar thoughts in regards to delayed consequences in her article for *The Daily Bread*. "As a child, I learned to behave properly when adults rewarded my good behavior and punished my bad behavior. This worked pretty well because the reward or punishment generally came quickly after the behavior, making the relationship between the cause and effect unmistakable. When I became an adult, however, life got more complex, and the consequences of my actions were not always immediate. When I behaved badly without getting in trouble for it, I began to think that it didn't matter to God what I did."[15]

Something similar happened to the children of Israel. When they disobeyed God and didn't suffer bad consequences right away, they said, "The Lord has forsaken the land, and the Lord does not see!" **Ezekiel 9:9 (NIV)**. They mistakenly believed that God had lost interest in them and didn't care about their behavior, but they were wrong. Weary of their waywardness, God said, "None of My words will be delayed any longer; whatever I say will be fulfilled." **Ezekiel 12:28 (NIV)**

We are all taught as kids not to touch a hot stove. Our parents demonstrate the stove is hot by pretending to touch a burner, then drawing their hand back in mock pain. The problem with the life lesson of the hot stove is that the stove isn't always on. Hence, there is a good chance that if a child accidentally or deliberately touches the burner he won't get burned. This leads to the child drawing one of two conclusions: He may think his parents were not telling the truth (surely you will not die for God knows...) or He may think he is invincible! Since the child wasn't immediately burned by the hot stove he believes there are no consequences at all.

Much like a hot stove, most parents warn their kids that hanging around the wrong crowd leads to trouble, that sex before marriage brings heartbreak and pain, and that getting high results in bad decisions. However, just as the enemy tempted Adam and Eve to doubt their Father's words, he will also tempt children to ignore their parents' wise advice, and goad them to touch the world to see if it is hot. He will delay the consequences of their actions in order to deceive them into believing the world is not hot and that there are no negative consequences to doing whatever they wish. That is why the first time they have sex, they probably won't get pregnant or get an STD, nor is it likely that they will get a DUI the first time they get drunk and hang with the wrong crowd. The enemy will delay the consequences of their actions because he wants to blind them to the high cost of the poor choices they have made.

Delaying consequences is a very deceptive strategy the enemy uses to lure us away from God's purpose for our lives and lull us into a spiritual numbness and apathy toward God's ways, direction and will. In many cases, we may even be deceived into thinking we are in God's will because if we weren't, things wouldn't be going so well for us. What deception!

In what areas have you been deceived into abusing God's grace?

Have delayed consequences enticed you to live life your way instead of God's way?

What decisions or actions have you been deceived into repeating because of delayed consequences?

12

Distraction

Let your eyes look directly forward, and your gaze be straight before you. Ponder the path of your feet; then all your ways will be sure. Do not swerve to the right or to the left; turn your foot away from evil.
Proverbs 4:25-27 (ESV)

Jonathan Mikael Raynes momentarily took his eyes off the road and swerved into oncoming traffic in an attempt to avoid hitting a stopped car in front of him. Instead, his F-150 collided head on with Miranda Hamilton's F-150. She was thrown from the truck and subsequently died from her injuries. She was only weeks from graduating from the University of South Alabama.

Over four days in court, the prosecution argued Raynes was fixated on his phone while driving, sending texts and instant messages, and visiting multiple social apps, including online dating sites. An information and technology specialist and digital forensic examiner for the FBI noted the last time Raynes "manipulated" his phone was 32 seconds before the first 911 call. Raynes was convicted of manslaughter and received a 10-year split sentence.[16]

Distracted driving is extremely dangerous and irresponsible. It places ourselves and others at risk. We have all witnessed drivers next to us on their phones, fixing their makeup, or even reading. Now, I have never been accused of fixing my makeup while driving, but on the other two infractions I would have to plead guilty.

What makes distracted driving so dangerous is the fact that we are not focused on our direction when driving safely and successfully to our destination. When we are distracted, we forget our surroundings, which impairs our ability to make good decisions. We become so fixated on a text, email or our appearance that our focus moves from our purpose, which is arriving safely, to something far less important that could potentially derail our purpose and life.

Google defines distraction as a thing that prevents someone from giving full attention to something else. For example, your phone messages may distract you from spending quality time with your family at the dinner table. Email can distract you from paying attention during a meeting. One negative thing can distract you from giving your attention to positive things such as the blessings you have. Your past failures may distract you from your current purposes and opportunities.

The enemy will attempt to deceive us through distraction. He seeks to distract us from God's blessings, love, presence and purpose for our lives. He wants to prevent us from giving our attention to God and focus on things that won't help us fulfill our purpose. He knows that we can only give our full attention to one person or one thing at a time, so he will send distractions our way to make sure we focus on anything *but* God. In his book, **Nehemiah: Learning to Lead**, Christian theologian James Montgomery Boice shares a baseball legend about overcoming distraction.

> *"There is a story involving Yogi Berra, the well-known catcher for the New York Yankees, and Hank Aaron, who at that time was the chief power hitter for the Milwaukee Braves. The teams were playing in the World Series, and as usual Yogi was keeping up his ceaseless chatter, intended to pep up his teammates on the one hand, and distract the Milwaukee batters on the other. As Aaron came to the plate, Yogi tried to distract him by saying, "Henry, you're holding the bat wrong. You're supposed to hold it so you can read the trademark." Aaron didn't say anything, but when the next pitch came he hit it into the*

left-field bleachers. After rounding the bases and tagging up at home plate, Aaron looked at Yogi Berra and said, "I didn't come up here to read." [17]

The enemy loves to trash-talk, to keep us distracted from our purpose. He knows he doesn't have to prevent you from accomplishing your purpose. All he has to do is distract you to keep you from pursuing it. He does this by getting you so focused on your daily routine, fears and capabilities that you forget you even have a purpose. Trash-talk is a tactic he uses to intimidate you and destroy your confidence. It's the enemy's way of discouraging you from making your best efforts. Athletes use it on a regular basis because it works. Check out some of these trash-talking lines athletes have used to undermine their opponents:

> *"When I retire, I'll get Ricky Hatton to wash my clothes and cut my lawn and buckle my shoes. Ricky Hatton ain't nothing but a fat man. I'm going to punch him in his beer belly. He ain't good enough to be my sparring partner."*
> ~ **Floyd Mayweather Jr.**

> *"I'm just looking around to see who's gonna finish second."*
> ~ **Larry Bird**

> *"What's the difference between a three-week-old puppy and a sportswriter? In six weeks, the puppy stops whining."*
> ~ **Mike Ditka**

> *"Kentucky has a heck of a punter, I know that."*
> ~ **Steve Spurrier**

> *"If my mother put on a helmet and shoulder pads and a uniform that wasn't the same as the one I was wearing, I'd run over her if she was in my way. And I love my mother."*
> ~ **Bo Jackson**

Make no mistake about it when your enemy speaks, he is talking trash. He always has and always will. He talks trash because he is full of lies and he knows it's the only thing he can do to stop you since Jesus made him a defeated foe. Thus his goal is to convince you that you are the defeated one in order to get you to stop trying or quit altogether. His plan is to keep you from your victory.

The enemy will distract you by goading you to focus on your problems instead of your purpose. He will get you focused on your inabilities instead of God's abilities. What makes this such an efficient strategy is that when we focus on our problems, we are blind to everything else. Inattentional blindness is a psychological phenomenon that occurs when a person is so focused on one thing, he cannot see anything else, though it's right in front of his face. Wikipedia describes inattentional blindness as "perceptual blindness caused by a psychological lack of attention that is not associated with actual vision defects or deficits[18]". It happens when a person finds it impossible to attend to all the stimuli in a given situation, and a temporary blindness effect takes place as a result, causing the person to fail to see objects that are not only noticeable, but important.

Inattentional blindness comes from focusing on one thing so much we don't see anything else. When we focus on what we don't have, we cannot see what we do have. When we focus on our weaknesses, we cannot see God's strength. When we focus on our past, we cannot see our future. When we focus on our failed dreams, we cannot see our future hope. When we focus on our pain, we cannot see our healing. When we focus on our circumstances, we cannot see Jesus.

In the previous chapter on patience, we talked about how Abram's wife, Sarai, could not get pregnant with the son God had promised them, so she told Abram to sleep with Hagar, her servant, so she could have his child. Anytime we try to fulfill God's plan on our own terms, it produces unforeseen consequences. Abram slept with Hagar who became pregnant and gave birth to a son named Ishmael. Abram and Hagar were excited by this news, but guess who was not? Sarai! Although her plan worked, it also forced her to face her failure, inabilities, and insecurities. Sarai had Abram send Hagar and Ishmael away. As we read the passage in Genesis, we find Hagar cast out, a single mother of a young son, alone, broken and poor. She is so poor that she cannot feed or care for young Ishmael.

> "When the water in the skin was gone, she put the child under one of the bushes. Then she went and sat down opposite him a good way off, about the distance of a bowshot, for she said, Let me not look on the death of the child. And as she sat opposite him, she lifted up her voice and wept. And God heard the voice of the boy, and the angel of God called to Hagar from heaven and said to her, What troubles you, Hagar? Fear not, for God has heard the voice of the boy where he is. Up! Lift up the boy, and hold him fast with your hand, for I will make him into a great nation. Then God opened her eyes, and she saw a well of water. And she went and filled the skin with water and gave the boy a drink." **Genesis 21:15-19**

Hagar laid Ishmael down because her heart would not allow her to watch him die a slow death of dehydration. What agony. She could hear her son crying, but could not help him. She would know when he was dead when the crying stopped.

It is in this heartbreaking moment that God shows up and encourages her not to be afraid, but to pick up the boy because He has a promise for her and Ishmael. God tells her Ishmael will not die, but will become the father of a great nation. If you are a single mother or were born into a non-traditional home let this encourage you. Ishmael was born to a servant girl. His mother was taken advantage of and they were both thrown to the wolves with no help in sight. It does not matter how your life begins, God has a purpose and a promise for you. He is a God of new beginnings.

God Helps Us See

What God does for Hagar is key to living out His purpose and plan for your life and preventing the enemy from disrupting that plan. God opened her eyes and helped her to see. I am not sure if her eyes were closed from crying over her dying son or from her own dehydration, fatigue and pain. All we know is that her eyes were so focused on her circumstances, they were closed to the solutions around her.

We all close our eyes from time to time. We get so focused on our shame that we cannot see our hope. We get so focused on how someone has offended or hurt us, we cannot see all the good they have done for us or joy they have brought into our lives. What about you? What have you focused on so much that you have closed your eyes to everything else in your life? Could you be so focused on the pain or abuse of your past that your eyes are closed to God and His help? Let God open your eyes and help you see!

What did Hagar see when God opened her eyes? Maybe she had to wipe tears away first, or maybe it took a minute to focus in the bright desert sunshine in order to clearly see her surroundings. All we know is that when God opened her eyes, the first thing she saw was a well of water. She saw the solution to her problem. Her son was dying from lack of water and now right in front of her was a full supply. God is a great and faithful provider who always provides us with a full supply to meet our needs. How is it that she could not see it? The enemy had distracted her by getting her so focused on her impending loss, she could not see God's provision, help and solution right in front of her. She was a victim of inattentional blindness.

The battle to walk in your purpose is one that requires focus and attention. The enemy seeks to steal your attention away from your God-created purpose and place it on activities that have no purpose and no eternal impact. Do you think there's any connection between our lives being busier than ever with attention-demanding luxuries and technology that produce increased frustration, depression, anxiety and suicide? I believe the increase is because we have allowed the enemy to distract us with things that steal our attention and focus away from God, keeping us from fulfilling His purpose for our lives.

The enemy seeks to distract us from being aware of the presence of God, which is everywhere. There is no place you can go to get away from the Holy Spirit. He is omnipresent, which means He is everywhere at all times. He is in every church, mosque and temple. He is at every football game, nightclub and bar. There's no cave, mountain crevice or sea depth where His presence cannot be found. King David said:

> *"Where shall I go from your Spirit? Or where shall I flee from your presence? If I ascend to heaven, you are there! If I make my bed in Sheol, you are there!"* **Psalms 139:7-8 (ESV)**

God's Spirit is everywhere! It is not a question of "if" He is present, it is only a question of if we are aware of His presence. The enemy cannot remove us from God's presence, but he will try to blind us to it. Paul says in **Romans 8:35-39 (ESV):**

> *"Who shall separate us from the love of Christ? Shall tribulation, or distress, or persecution, or famine, or nakedness, or danger, or sword? As it is written, For your sake we are being killed all the day long; we are regarded as sheep to be slaughtered. No, in all these things we are more than conquerors through him who loved us. For I am sure that neither death nor life, nor angels nor rulers, nor things pres-*

ent nor things to come, nor powers, nor height nor depth, nor anything else in all creation, will be able to separate us from the love of God in Christ Jesus our Lord."

No, the enemy cannot separate us from God's love or His presence. It does not matter what is going on in your life, how deep your sin or how tragic your failure. God's love is always directed toward us. Think about that. In your darkest days, when you were caught up in your worst sin, and in that very moment you embraced such despicable, evil and sinful imaginings, God was there and He loved you. When you were far away from God, or hated Him and despised His ways, when you loved sin and rejected Him, God was there and He loved you. When you were drunk, or on drugs, had an abortion, were in jail or practicing homosexuality, God was there and He loved you. When you were an atheist, muslim or satanist, God was there and He loved you. He loved you in your darkest hour, but how much more does His love shine upon us when we see and respond to His presence?

The enemy knows this truth. Do you? Do you truly realize that the presence of God is with you in every moment, decision, action and reaction? This truth should change the way we live. We live in the presence of a Holy God 24 hours a day, seven days a week, and 365 days a year — and 366 days during Leap Year.

Since the enemy knows he cannot remove us from the presence of God, his only option is to distract us from God's presence. He wants to take our attention and focus off of God. During worship he will distract us by having us focus on the people around us, the volume or style of the music. During prayer he will distract us with the day's task list, meetings or activities. Distraction robs us of the intimacy we long for with God.

Distraction is what leads us to cry out: "Where is God?" or "Why have you forsaken me?" God does not come or go. He is constant and He is with you. The problem of God's presence is never on His side of the equation. He is the constant variable. We, on the other hand, are the inconstant variable. When we feel like God is far from us or distant, it is you and I who are distant. We have moved our attention and focus from God to other things that we have deemed to be more important to us than the presence of God. **We give our attention to what is important to us.** Our hearts focus on what we value. The enemy will distract us by leading us to believe that our jobs, finances, hobbies, education, kids, marriage, politics, activities, fitness, dreams, etc. are more valuable at the moment than the presence of God.

If God seems distant right now, ask yourself these questions:

1. What am I giving my focus, attention and heart to right now in this season of life?
2. Have I been distracted from the direction God wants me to go in life?
3. Have I allowed the enemy to trash-talk so much that I have lost my focus on what God says about me and my purpose?
4. Have I allowed the enemy to distract me from God's strength by focusing on my weaknesses?
5. Am I trying to arrive at my divine destiny while living distracted?

If you answered yes to any of these questions, today is the day to turn your phone off, place both hands on the steering wheel of your life and direct your focus squarely on God!

13

Authenticity

Examine yourselves to see if your faith is genuine. Test yourselves.
Surely you know that Jesus Christ is among you; if not,
you have failed the test of genuine faith.
2 Corinthians 13:5 (ESV)

There is a classic story about a young Chinese boy who wanted to help provide for his family by finding and selling jade. The only problem was he didn't know what real jade looked like or where to find it. He heard about a great teacher and jade expert with a keen eye for spotting fakes, so he went to study with him.

When the young boy met the gentle, old teacher, he did not give him a lesson. He simply placed a piece of jade into his hand and told him to hold it tight. Then, he began to talk about philosophy, men, women, the sun and almost everything under it. After an hour, he took back the stone and sent the boy home. The teacher repeated this procedure for several weeks. Meanwhile, the boy became increasingly frustrated. When would he be taught about jade? He didn't want to learn about philosophy or life. He wanted to learn about jade. However, he was too polite to question the wisdom of his venerable teacher. One day, when the old man put a stone into his hands, the boy cried out instinctively, "That's not jade!"

This boy learned what he desired to know through the lessons of everyday life, which is how the Holy Spirit teaches us. Even when we don't feel like we are learning what we want or need to know, He is always guiding and teaching us truth. God knows that the easiest way to prevent deception from infecting our lives is to have us become so acquainted with what is authentic that counterfeits are easily spotted. The more we familiarize ourselves with His truths, the easier and quicker we will be able to spot anything that is a lie. We will be like the young Chinese boy and shout, "That's not true!"[19]

Get Real

We prevent ourselves from being deceived when we live by the principle of "keeping it real." This means we focus our hearts and minds on truth, not fearing what others may think, but instead being most concerned with what God thinks. It is critical to our spiritual health and journey that we be honest with ourselves and others and conduct our relationships with transparency and authenticity.

The easiest people to deceive are the people who are not true to themselves. In many cases we are our own worst enemies. We pretend things are fine when they are not. We think higher of ourselves than we ought. We put on masks in order to hide our feelings from others. There's a mask we put on in order to appear to live up to the spiritual expectations of church friends. There's a happy mask we put on to hide our pain and struggles. There's a success mask we put on so friends and coworkers think well of us.

The problem with masks is that they prevent others from seeing you clearly. When you hide the truth from people who care about you, they cannot love and support you when you need it most. It is only when we are open, honest and real with people and allow them to see what we are going through that they can help us in our time of need.

Do you remember when Halloween costumes came with a molded plastic mask with an elastic band straight from the pits of hell that was intended to hold the mask on your head? Those masks typically had two tiny holes in the eyes to see through, but they were so small, the only thing visible was the inside of the mask. I vividly remember having to listen for the sound of candy dropping into my bag because I couldn't see it. Eventually the media and parents began talking about how unsafe masks were for kids who were essentially blind while navigating neighborhood streets in the dark.

The masks we wear as adults are even more unsafe than the plastic ones we wore as children. Our eternal purpose, spiritual and mental health, dreams and legacy are at stake. We will never be able to overcome temptation if we willfully choose to present a lie. We will never have deep and meaningful relationships if people do not know who we really are. We will never overcome temptation and receive comfort if people cannot see what is really going on in our lives. God will not bless our masks. He will only bless the "real" us.

The Deception of Focusing on the Fake

We all have a desire to want to know how to spot a lie. We study all different types of fakes, false gospels, counterfeit spirits and the lies in the news and social media. However, I believe that the enemy can use this desire to gets us so fixated on looking for counterfeits that we spend more time absorbed by exposing lies than in exposing our hearts and minds to the truth of God's Word. As Jesus told us in John 8:32: *"If you continue in My word, you are truly My disciples. Then you will know the truth, and the truth will set you free."*

It is spending time meditating on the truth of God's word that sets us free, not consuming ourselves with spotting fakes. Some of us are not free because we devote all of our time and attention to spotting lies and spend very little time holding God's truth in our hands and examining it in-depth until we know it down deep in our souls.

In John MacArthur's book *Reckless Faith* he states, *"Federal agents don't learn to spot counterfeit money by studying the counterfeits. They study genuine bills until they master the look of the real thing. Then when they see the bogus money they recognize it."* Christian author, Tim Challies had heard this principle many times and decided to visit a federal agent at the Bank of Canada to see if it was in fact, true. Here is what he observed: *"Training in identifying counterfeit currency begins with studying genuine money. There are certain identifying characteristics that are added to each bill printed by the Bank of Canada. These characteristics are necessarily difficult to reproduce. Some are intended to stump the casual counterfeiter, armed with no more than a scanner and color laser printer, and some will stump the more serious counterfeiter, even if armed with expensive, high-tech equipment."* [20]

The federal agents would have been called Bereans in the Bible. The Bereans are famous in the book of Acts for examining the messages preached by Paul and Silas to see if they were in alignment with the truth of Scripture. Because of their diligence in faithfully studying God's word, the Bereans were well-acquainted with the truth, and therefore could not be easily deceived.

> *"Now these Jews were more noble than those in Thessalonica; they received the word with all eagerness, examining the Scriptures daily to see if these things were so."*
> **Acts 17:11 (ESV)**

Challies shared that the four techniques agents use in learning to recognize the authenticity of currency are "touch, tilt, look at, and look through." Agents look at a bill to observe its features or lack thereof. Then, they hold it and get a feel for it, tilting it to observe it from various perspectives. Finally, they hold it up to the light and look through it. Although looks can be deceiving, many times the truth is hidden in plain sight. I believe that many times we miss the truth of God's word and plan for our lives because we haven't spent any time examining it.

I recently spent two and half days in prayer at a silent retreat at a Trappist monastery. I had never been to mass or a Catholic service so I was a little scared of monks and nuns, perhaps from watching too many movies set in the Dark Ages. Anyway I stepped way out of my comfort zone. I knew that I was going away to pray and listen to God speak. I prayed for my family and friends, the church staff, elders and members, my life and ministry, and even for the people who would read this book. That's right, you are an answer to my prayers.

One thing I was hoping for was a loud and clear word from the Lord for each person and topic for which I was praying. God did speak clearly to me in many areas, but it was not in the way I thought He would. Instead of having a revelatory experience, He changed my focus and attention from asking Him to reveal truth to me, to instead looking more deeply into the truth He had already set before me.

Truth Is Simple. Deception Is Complex.

Do you know why police officers ask the same questions repeatedly during interrogation or when you get pulled over for a traffic stop? If you are telling the truth you will repeat the same answer the same way each time. If you are not telling the truth your answer will vary with each repetition of the question. Why? Truth is simple. It doesn't take thought and great effort to repeat. Conversely, lies are intricately crafted. They require management and hard work in order to recall them with consistency. As American author, Mark Twain once said, "If you tell the truth, you don't have to remember anything."

In the same way federal agents pick up currency to experience its weight, we can experience the weight of God's truth by regularly picking up His word, reading it and holding onto the truths we find inside. In his letter to Timothy, Paul challenges him (and us) to become skilled in handling the truth.

> *"Do your best to present yourself to God as one approved,*
> *a worker who has no need to be ashamed,*
> *rightly handling the word of truth."*
> **2 Timothy 2:15 (ESV)**

We have the gift of God's Word, the Bible, and the gift of the author, the Holy Spirit, to guide us in handling the truth. The Bible is truth and when it is handled correctly it becomes our greatest weapon against the lies of the enemy and a faithful guide for understanding God's will and purpose for our lives. When we mishandle God's word by failing to study it regularly or ignoring it altogether, we miss His purpose for our lives. Truth does set us free, but we must read, believe, know and apply God's truth before we can experience the promised freedom it holds for us.

Biblical Illiteracy

It is no wonder that deception is so rampant in our culture and churches. When people and churches believe truth is what they feel or desire instead of what God says, they have not handled His Word correctly - if they have handled it at all.

Biblical illiteracy is at an all time high. According to research, only 20 percent of Americans have ever read the entire Bible. The same survey of biblical literacy in America also found that only 22 percent of people read a little bit of the Bible each day, whereas 35 percent never pick up a Bible at all. The remainder of those surveyed tend to open the Bible at random to look something up "when they need to."

If you're thinking, "sure, that's America in general, but people who attend church regularly are likely more engaged with God's word.," unfortunately, theologian Ed Stetzer's research on American church attendees' engagement with the Bible disagrees. His study found that of this group:

- 19% read the Bible every day
- 18% rarely or never read the Bible
- 22% read the Bible one or more times a month
- 14% read the Bible once a week
- 25% read the Bible a few times a week[20]

People are listening to sermons online or from their preacher on Sunday, but they are not reading their Bibles. If they did, they would recognize that many churches are not teaching or preaching the Bible. Instead they give audience acceptable motivational talks, featuring life and moral instructions with just a light sprinkling of the Word of God thrown in for a touch of integrity. When churches no longer preach God's Word and Truth, it results in the cultural shift we are experiencing now, where people believe truth is relative to the individual. It's the popular and poisonous "you do you" and "live your own truth" philosophy.

Singer and songwriter Sara Groves captured the American epidemic of biblical illiteracy brilliantly in her song, *The Word*.

I've done every devotional
Been every place emotional
Trying to hear a new word from God
And I think it's very odd,
That while I attempt to help myself
My Bible sits upon my shelf
With every promise
I could ever need

And the Word was
And the Word is
And the Word will be

People are getting fit for Truth
Like they're buying a new tailored suit
Does it fit across the shoulders
Does it fade when it gets older
We throw ideas that aren't in style
In the Salvation Army pile
And search for something more to meet our needs

And the Word I need
Is the Word that was
Who put on flesh to dwell with us.
In the beginning

When we no longer handle the truth, Satan has the upper hand because he knows more about the Bible than most believers do. In Matthew 4:6, when Satan tempted Jesus to throw himself off the temple mount, he quoted scripture out of context as part of his ploy. However, take note of how Jesus defeated the enemy in his tactics. In all three recorded temptations, Jesus responded to Satan by saying, "It is written…" and then He would use the Word to gain the victory over Satan.

When we fail to seek God in His word, our enemy can easily deceive us because we are no longer familiar with truth. As God states in the beginning of Hosea 4:6, *"My people are destroyed for lack of knowledge…"* Our fundamental lack of reading the Bible has created a devastating lack of knowledge and understanding of the truth. We are unable to declare, "It is written…" when presented with a deception because we don't know the truth.

When we are not familiar with truth, we cling to half-truths and

deceptions. We live in a world where truth is often taken out of context in order to suit our needs. Because people don't have a contextual understanding of truth, they cannot understand the big picture of God's will and plan for their lives. When the only scripture being read is via Twitter posts or Tim Tebow's eye black, how can we possibly expect to live the lives Christ died to give us? We can and must do better at handling the truth. God's plan for our lives, His mission upon this earth, and our walk with Jesus is depending upon it.

Truth Check-Up

In the Spirit of truth and authenticity, ask yourself the following questions:

How am I handling the truth? Am I pursuing God's word with passion or passivity?

Do I apply God's word to my life? Do I let it determine my opinions, values and decisions?

Am I reading it in context, or do I read to affirm my own context?

> *My child, pay attention to what I say.*
> *Listen carefully to my words.*
> *Don't lose sight of them.*
> *Let them penetrate deep into your heart,*
> *for they bring life to those who find them,*
> *and healing to their whole body.*
> **Proverbs 4:20-22 (NLT)**

God's Word is life. If you are not currently reading His Word, stop reading this book right now and start handling the truth by beginning a Bible reading plan. You can go to YouVersion and start a plan now, or you can check out the Bible reading plan resources in the back of this book. If you take care to read and obey God's truth, His truth will take care of you.

14
Isolation

The LORD God said, "It is not good for the man to be alone.
I will make a helper suitable for him."
Genesis 2:18 (NIV)

"You have a very rare and extremely contagious condition," the doctor told his patient.

"We're going to put you in an isolation unit, where you'll be on a diet of pancakes and pizza."

"Will pancakes and pizza cure my condition?"

"No," replied the doctor. "They're the only things we can slip under the door." [22]

Isolation limits what God can get to us. When we choose to hide or dwell in isolation, we cut ourselves off from the very blessings and resources that we are praying for. God often answers our prayers through the people in our lives. He sends provision, comfort, guidance and encouragement through others. When we cut ourselves off from others due to pride, pain or fear, we cut ourselves off from the resources we need to overcome temptation and the tactics of our enemy to live victorious lives. Isolation is a tactic of the enemy to keep you away from the blessings of God. This is why God's plan is centered around community and relationships.

Christianity is not a religion for individuals, but for community. The entire Bible is a story of relationship and community. God knows that we need Him and we need each other. We cannot fulfill our purpose, walk in victory or live abundant lives by ourselves because it is not God's will. God calls us to walk together.

> *Two people are better off than one, for they can help each other succeed. If one person falls, the other can reach out and help. But someone who falls alone is in real trouble. Likewise, two people lying close together can keep each other warm. But how can one be warm alone? A person standing alone can be attacked and defeated, but two can stand back-to-back and conquer. Three are even better, for a triple-braided cord is not easily broken.*
> **Ecclesiastes 4:9-12 (NLT)**

If we want to get acquainted with truth and overcome the enemy's deceptive tactics, we cannot solely depend on our own perspective. None of us are wise enough, smart enough, holy enough, mature enough or strong enough to overcome deception by ourselves. In fact, the moment you think you can, you are already deceived.

Your perspective is limited to your experiences, knowledge, personality and abilities. If you live your life from a single angle of perspective, the enemy will be able to easily deceive you by using unfamiliar angles. That's why it is imperative we seek wise counsel in the perspectives of others, who love God and His Word. Godly friends will help you gain a better view of your situation, by filtering it through their understanding of His will and ways. They can help you discern the voice of God, see the truth and help you grow in your knowledge of God's Word. One of God's greatest gifts to you is the fresh perspective of a trustworthy friend. Proverbs has much to say about the benefits of being transparent with others and seeking their wisdom on the various situations in our lives.

> *As iron sharpens iron, so a friend sharpens a friend.*
> **Proverbs 27:17 (NLT)**
>
> *Without counsel plans fail, but with*
> *many advisers they succeed.*
> **Proverbs 15:22 (ESV)**

Why do our plans fail without counsel? Because we lack perspective. When we don't have anyone to help us see things clearly, our viewpoint and thinking is akin to tunnel vision. We barrel down the tracks of our lives convinced we don't need counsel because we think our point of view is fine, but we are woefully deceived. The greatest deception occurs when you no longer think you can be deceived.

Why do plans succeed with many advisers? Because the greater the counselors, the greater the perspectives, wisdom and insights.

Major corporations and even governments know and understand this principle. They apply its wisdom to their organizations by electing a board of directors, typically comprised of seasoned professionals with deep experience and knowledge of both success and failure. The ultimate task of all such boards is to help a business grow, thrive and make better decisions by equipping leaders with expert insights from people who are adept at navigating challenges and opportunities.

If companies, whose purposes are temporal, apply the biblical principle of many advisers in order to ensure their success, why don't followers of Jesus, whose purposes are eternal, apply the same principle? Why do these corporations take stock value more seriously than we take eternal value?

If you want to live a life that overcomes deception and other tactics of the enemy, I strongly encourage you to build your own personal board of directors. I first heard about this principle years ago from a message that Pastor Ed Young Jr. of Fellowship Church in Dallas preached. It was a teaching that not only changed my life, it increased my ability to make wiser decisions greatly. The principle is simply inviting people into your life to help you navigate God's will and make better decisions. I recommend inviting people who have already traversed the path you are currently on, or who are successful in areas you would like to be successful.

My personal board of directors is comprised of close friends that I respect, love and trust. Each one is successful in areas I want to be successful, such as being a husband, father, leader, pastor and disciple of Christ. Whenever I need accountability or advice for a decision in one of those areas, I go to my personal board of directors. Over the years, the insights and perspectives of these men and women have made me a better father, husband, pastor and follower of Jesus. They have prevented me from making unwise decisions that I would have made without their perspective. They have helped prepare me for new seasons of marriage and parenting. They have shared wisdom from their experiences that have helped me lead my wife and children with love and grace. They have helped me discern God's will in times of major life-changing decisions.

To establish your own personal board of directors, you don't have to send official invitations or conduct monthly meetings. Just select a few people whose success you would like to emulate in your life. Then, invite them to lunch or simply call and ask for their advice. Most people will be honored to offer wise counsel, so make sure you respect their time and investment in your life by applying their wisdom to your situation. Think about the areas of life you want to overcome temptation or gain a victory and then ask the Lord to help you identify people who would be willing to speak wisdom into your life.

The Chairman of Your Personal Board of Directors

It is amazing how evident the truth is and how quickly deception is exposed when we hold it up to the Light (Jesus). When we seek Him in our decisions and bring Him all of our emotions, dreams, fears, concerns and plans, He is faithful to show us what is true, what is false and the way we should go.

> *"No one after lighting a lamp covers it with a jar or puts it under a bed, but puts it on a stand, so that those who enter may see the light. For nothing is hidden that will not be made manifest, nor is anything secret that will not be known and come to light."*
> **Luke 8:16-17 (ESV)**

Everything is brought to light at some point. Every lie of the devil. Every counterfeit plan and scheme. Every ill-purposed action, motive and hidden agenda. How much better would our lives be if we brought everything to the Light instead of going our own way, becoming deceived and needing Jesus to expose the lies we have believed so that we can be receive healing and walk in wholeness. What if instead of getting caught in sin, we brought our temptations into the Light? After all, it will all be exposed at some point anyway. What if we consistently overcame temptation and deception because we were ruthless in holding up our desires, emotions, decision, and actions to the Light first? The idea of you seeking God first in all things makes the enemy tremble. He knows there is no deception in the Light! He only has the power to deceive us in the dark. That's why he wants us to hide from the Light.

One of the great deceptions the enemy attempts to convince us of is that we should be afraid to bring things into the Light. He tells us that if our sin is exposed, we will lose everything and that if we bring our temptations to the Light, God will judge us for it. He convinces us that if we share our struggles with someone else, they will look at us differently, or if we bring things from the dark to the light, it will have negative effects. Nothing could be further from the truth.

It is only when we confess sin by bringing it to Light that we experience the power of forgiveness. As my close friend Dave Deerman has said, "Sin grows when it's hidden. Freedom happens when sin is exposed to the Light." It is only when we bring our temptations to Light with others that we gain accountability, experience freedom and take hold of the power to overcome those things that seek to destroy us.

What are you keeping in the dark that needs to be brought to the Light? Remember the enemy only has power in the dark.

15

Disobedience

Everyone who keeps living in sin also practices disobedience.
In fact, sin is disobedience.
1 John 3:4 (ISV)

Sin Is Not a Mistake. Sin Is a Decision.

Every day my mailbox is full of bills, advertisements, and credit card offers from Visa, MasterCard, Discover, and American Express. They market themselves in a way that lets me know that they can't wait to help me live out all of my dreams. With their help, I can afford to go to Bora Bora. I can deliver an embarrassment of riches to family at Christmas. I can buy my wife, Toyia, a bigger diamond and my kids the latest Apple devices. Obviously, the credit card company is only trying to help, right? Wrong! Credit card companies want to provide you with the fleeting happiness of instant gratification. In exchange for this momentary thrill, you enjoy a lifetime of crippling indebtedness to their benevolence, and empower their executives to live largely off of your inability to wait.

The front end of credit offers are designed to appear smart by offering you a few months to pay them back without interest. It's a hook that works because people assume they will take advantage of the offer, not realizing it was designed to take advantage of them. Statistics prove that most people, despite good intentions, will never meet the offer's "free" terms, which means they will pay exorbitant interest on their purchases. What's worse is that once the average 23 percent interest begins, people end up paying far more for something than it is worth. In fact, some people will pay for an item they buy on credit multiple times in interest before they ever pay off the item itself.

One of the ways I teach people about credit is by asking them if they want to buy $100 from me for $123? Naturally, most people look at me like I'm crazy before saying, "No!" When I ask them why not, they usually respond that it is dumb to buy money. But when you use credit you are actually buying money. Why would anyone do this? Simple, we have a desire we want to fulfill and we don't have the means to fulfill it, so we let someone give us the means to fill it ourselves.

When we insist on having things our way, we end up disobeying God and getting outside of His plans for our lives. If you desire something that you don't have the ability to fulfill, seek God about it first. He is your provider and the one who fulfills your desires. Every time you allow the enemy to deceive you into thinking you can find fulfillment on your own or through other means, you lose. His offer to you of buy now and pay later is always a bad deal.

The Paradox Principle of Sacrifice

There is a principle in psychology called the "Paradox Principle of Sacrifice." The principle, as stated by author Rory Vaden is: "Easy short-term choices lead to difficult long-term consequences, meanwhile difficult short-term choices lead to easy long-term consequences."[23] An example of the Paradox Principle everyone can relate to is the decision to go to a drive thru and grab a hamburger, fries and soda when we are hungry. Although a quick and easy way to satisfy our desire for food, it's a decision that when repeated often leads to long-term negative consequences, such as obesity, heart problems, high blood pressure, etc. The alternative, which is to choose to go to the grocery store and buy food so we can pack a healthy lunch requires more effort up front, but in the long run, this choice leads to a healthier body and finances, a much easier long-term consequence to deal with.

It is easy to get a credit card and take your family on a dream vacation to Disney World for a week. It is hard to suffer through years of financial stress while shortchanging your family of quality time with you, while you work more and more in order to pay it all back — with interest. It is difficult to save money for a dream vacation, but this choice comes with the easy long-term consequences of financial freedom and peace.

Most good decisions seem more difficult in the beginning, whereas most bad ones appear extremely quick and easy. When we disobey God, we choose to apply for credit with our enemy. Sin and rebellion both offer immediate pleasure, but when the pleasure fades, we are left with a horrific debt that is back-loaded with interest. As Christian theologian and apologist Ravi Zacharias says, "Sin will take you farther than you want to go, keep you longer than you want to stay, and cost you more than you want to pay." We see the high cost of disobedience in the story of Adam and Eve. They saw something they wanted immediately, and chose to listen to the enemy instead of relying on what God had told them. They took what they wanted because they didn't want to wait for God to provide.

We have got to change the way we view sin. It is truly a matter of life and death. Our culture and many churches teach that sin is simply a mistake. They dilute the truth about sin by saying, "none of us is perfect." Although it is true that none of us is perfect and we all make mistakes, no one should continue living a life filled with sin and assume there will be no consequences. When we continue to sin as if it's no big deal, we don't honor God, we abuse the grace and blood of Jesus, and we disqualify ourselves from fulfilling God's purposes and receiving His blessings. Paul makes this abundantly clear in several of his letters.

Dear friends, if we deliberately continue sinning after we have received knowledge of the truth, there is no longer any sacrifice that will cover these sins. There is only the terrible expectation of God's judgment and the raging fire that will consume his enemies. For anyone who refused to obey the law of Moses was put to death without mercy on the testimony of two or three witnesses. Just think how much worse the punishment will be for those who have trampled on the Son of God, and have treated the blood of the covenant, which made us holy, as if it were common and unholy, and have insulted and disdained the Holy Spirit who brings God's mercy to us. **Hebrews 10:26-29 (NLT)**

> Well then, should we keep on sinning so that
> God can show us more and more of his
> wonderful grace? Of course not! Since we have
> died to sin, how can we continue to live in it?
> **Romans 6:1 (NLT)**

A mistake is a minor error in your judgment, such as misspelling a word during the essay portion of a test. Sin is taking your eyes off your own test and copying the answers of the person sitting next to you. It is an intentional decision to disobey.

> So whoever knows the right thing to do
> and fails to do it, for him it is sin.
> **James 4:17 (ESV)**

Sin Is Disobedience

We sin when we choose to disobey God's law, ways and will. Sin is knowing the right thing to do and choosing to do the wrong thing instead. Yes, there are a lot of variables that may influence our decision to sin, such as ignorance or deception, but our excuse for why we chose to do wrong will not get us a hall pass with God. To God, all sin is disobedience.

In 1 Kings 13, there is a story of a young prophet sent by God to tell the people that the altar in Israel would be torn in two and the ashes spilled on the ground. When the King heard this declaration, he reached out his hand to seize the prophet and arrest him, but it shriveled immediately and at the same time the altar broke in two and the ashes poured out on the ground, just as the young man had prophesied. Upon seeing his useless arm, the king begged the prophet to intercede for him and he did and God immediately healed the king's arm. The king then invited the prophet to the palace to receive a gift and eat with him, but God had told the prophet, 'Don't eat a crumb, don't drink a drop, and don't go back the way you came' **(1 Kings 13:8, MSG)**, so the prophet declined the king's offer and left by a different road.

An old prophet in the town heard about the young prophet and went in search of him. When he found him, he invited him to come eat with him. The young prophet declined telling him that God had told him not to eat, drink, or return the way he came. Then, the old prophet lied and said, "I am also a prophet, just like you. And an angel came to me with a message from God: 'Bring him home with you, and give him a good meal!'" But the old prophet was lying. Unfortunately, the young prophet went and ate dinner with the old prophet against God's will. While eating, the old prophet prophesied to the young prophet:

> "God's word to you: You disobeyed God's command; you didn't keep the strict orders your God gave you; you came back and sat down to a good meal in the very place God told you, 'Don't eat a crumb; don't drink a drop.' For that you're going to die far from home and not be buried in your ancestral tomb." **1 Kings 13:20-22, (MSG)**

When the young prophet left the old prophet's house, a lion met him on the road and killed him. The young prophet did not intend to disobey

God. He had been faithful to God's will and word until he was deceived by an older more mature prophet. Sadly, he trusted the old prophet's relationship with God more than his own relationship with God. Yes, he was deceived by someone who should have known better, but God was not concerned with why he disobeyed, He was concerned that he disobeyed.

We have to learn to see sin and disobedience through the eyes of God instead of through our own eyes. God sees sin much differently than we do and views disobedience more seriously than we do. Let's look at how God groups sins together.

> They were filled with all manner of unrighteousness, evil, covetousness, malice. They are full of envy, murder, strife, deceit, maliciousness. They are gossips, slanderers, haters of God, insolent, haughty, boastful, inventors of evil, disobedient to parents, foolish, faithless, heartless, ruthless.
> **Romans 1:29-31 (ESV)**

> Or do you not know that the unrighteous will not inherit the kingdom of God? Do not be deceived: neither the sexually immoral, nor idolaters, nor adulterers, nor men who practice homosexuality, nor thieves, nor the greedy, nor drunkards, nor revilers, nor swindlers will inherit the kingdom of God. **1 Corinthians 6:9-10 (ESV)**

> Now the works of the flesh are evident: sexual immorality, impurity, sensuality, idolatry, sorcery, enmity, strife, jealousy, fits of anger, rivalries, dissensions, divisions, envy, drunkenness, orgies, and things like these. I warn you, as I warned you before, that those who do such things will not inherit the kingdom of God.
> **Galatians 5:19-21 (ESV)**

- Unrighteousness
- Covetousness
- Malice
- Murder
- Deceit
- Gossip
- Slander
- Haughtiness
- Pride
- Disobedience to parents
- Sexual immorality
- Idolatry
- Adultery
- Homosexuality
- Theft
- Greed
- Drunkenness
- Revelry
- Swindlers
- Sensuality
- Impurity
- Sorcery
- Strife
- Jealousy
- Anger
- Rivalries
- Dissension
- Division
- Orgies

God puts gossip in the same category as murder and views teenage rebellion to be as evil as orgies. He sees armed robbery the same way He sees jealousy. Obviously, we have a different way of seeing sin than God does, but why? It is because God knows that all sin is serious, not just the ones with legal consequences. He sees the beginning from the end, and He knows that all sin results in death - death to dreams, hopes, destinies, our spirits, and ultimately our bodies and souls.

> For the wages of sin is death, but the free gift of God is eternal life through Christ Jesus our Lord. **Romans 6:23 (NLT)**

We are deceived when we believe God thinks and acts like we do. This is one of the trickiest deceptions of all, but a few signs to help you identify whether or not you are laboring under this misconception in your life are when you find yourself believing, saying and acting on statements, like:

- *God knows me and He understands my sin.*

- *God is loving and merciful, so He is okay with
  me continually disobeying.*

- *God is a Father, who just wants me to be myself and be happy.*

- *When I sin, I'll just ask for forgiveness.*

- *God knows what I'm like and His expectation is just for
  me to do my best.*

- *God knows everything. He knew I was going to sin, and
  He's already forgiven me.*

The root lie in all of these scenarios is a self-deception in which we take a comforting and genuine quality of God's character (i.e. His love, mercy, fatherhood, compassion, kindness, goodness, etc.) and we apply it to our beliefs as a way to excuse ourselves from submitting to His will and ways, which are always holy, righteous, pure, just and truthful. We give our flesh a donut instead of discipline and mistakenly believe, "God thinks just like I do, and I know how I would respond to me." In reality, when we brush off sin like it's no big deal, we undermine grace. We twist our theology and wield scripture out of context in order to mold it into a more palatable god of our own making. This god never dislikes anything we do, nor has any real expectations of us at all. Our created god reflects our own desires and ways and is not driven to serve the real, living and holy God. It is an idol that is weak in the areas we are weak and strong in the areas we are strong; thus, there is no real need to change in order to become like God or please Him. Believing that God thinks like we do is a lie that silences our consciences and allows us to take the broad path to destruction without feeling guilty. Essentially, when we stop following

Christ and instead expect Him to follow us and bless or overlook whatever we choose to do, we are in grave danger — quite literally.

> "For my thoughts are not your thoughts, neither are your
> ways my ways," declares the Lord. "As the heavens are
> higher than the earth, so are my ways higher than your
> ways and my thoughts than your thoughts."
> **Isaiah 55:8-9 (ESV)**

Sin Is Rebellion

When you choose to go your own way, you are rebelling against your holy King and His Kingdom. There are only two true kingdoms in all of creation: God's Kingdom and the kingdom of darkness. God's Kingdom is established on His character, will and glory. It is a Kingdom of light, hope, order, love and holiness. The kingdom of darkness is established on our character, will and glory. It is a kingdom of self-love, self-gratification and self-centeredness. It is a kingdom of chaos because everyone is seeking their own throne and glory. By nature, it is wholly evil because we live our lives according to our own standards instead of God's holy standards. There is no middle ground between these two kingdoms. You are either in one or the other.

Sin is an active rebellion against God's Kingdom in an attempt to set up our own. It's a campaign to be our own king with our own rules and decrees. What's more, like Satan himself, the originator of sin, our rebellion seeks partners in crime and tries to persuade people to join us in our kingdom. We forget that: "The earth is the Lord's, and everything in it. The world and all its people belong to him." (Psalm 24:1, NLT). Thus in our arrogance, we attempt to build our own palace using the real King's supplies. Theologian, R.C. Sproul said, "Sin is cosmic treason." Sproul then expounded, "What I meant by that statement was that even the slightest sin that a creature commits against his Creator does violence to the Creator's holiness, His glory, and His righteousness. Every sin, no matter how seemingly insignificant, is an act of rebellion against the sovereign God who reigns and rules over us and as such is an act of treason against the cosmic King."[24]

We are either a submitted servant in God's Kingdom, who embraces His ways, or we are an active rebel against Him, who rejects His ways. Each sin we commit is like a brick we use to build our own little kingdom. As we hide out in the house that sin built, we hope that God does not notice the new building project. Our highest aim is to finish doing whatever we want with our lives, bodies and decisions without getting caught by the King. In doing so, we cause more damage to ourselves than His Kingdom. His Kingdom will never be overthrown, but ours will be. A kingdom divided against itself will not stand.

> Jesus knew their thoughts and said to them, "Every kingdom divided against itself will be ruined, and every city or household divided against itself will not stand."
> **Matthew 12:25 (NIV)**

Sin is a serious matter. In fact, God's eternal timeline is marked by it. In Genesis, the world began with perfect holiness and intimacy between God and man. Then sin enters the world and separates man from God. So catastrophic is the devastation of sin and death that God must use the blood of His own Son, Jesus, as a perfect sacrifice to atone for sin and restore an intimate relationships between himself, a holy God, and us, His people.

> It's your sins that have cut you off from God. Because of your sins, he has turned away and will not listen anymore. **Isaiah 59:2 (NLT)**

If sin is such an important issue with God that He used His most precious resource to take care of it, why isn't it serious to us? I believe the reason we are not serious about sin is because we are not serious about God. If we were wholly committed to Him, we would be ruthless in eradicating anything that separated us from Him.

Sadly, the trouble most people have in overcoming sin is that they care more about themselves than God. We seek God's hand, but not His face. We receive Jesus for our personal benefits without realizing it is our Holy King who is receiving us, the former rebels, into His Kingdom. Our worship is centered around our wants, needs and pains instead of around the throne of God and His glory. When we get serious about God, we will get serious about our sin and stop attempting to serve God as a means to serve ourselves.

The kryptonite that foils the enemy's plan to entice us to sin is obedience. Holiness is forsaking evil and cleaving to God. Disobedience is forsaking God and cleaving to evil. As we abide in Jesus and His word, and lay hold of His promises, His blood, and its work in our lives, we gain strength in our commitment to obey God. We are better able to recognize the tactics of the enemy, flee from sin, and pursue an obedient lifestyle.

> So flee youthful passions and pursue righteousness, faith, love, and peace, along with those who all on the Lord from a pure heart. **2 Timothy 2:22 (ESV)**

One of the reasons many people struggle with obedience is because they make it about rules and regulations instead of a heart-to-heart relationship with God. They appear to be concerned with determining what is sin and what is not; however, their real priority is not setting a boundary, but seeing how close to sin it's possible to get without sinning. It's like little kids in the backseat of a car drawing an invisible line between themselves and saying, "This is my space and this is yours." Immediately both kids try to occupy as much space as possible without touching each other. We do the same thing with sin. We draw lines where we believe one side is sinful and the other side is holy. Then, we get as close to the line as we can while trying to stay on the right side. Adam and Eve had this problem. Instead of choosing to walk in a close and obedient relationship with God, they wanted to define what was good and what was evil.

Plotting to draw lines between good and evil is another foolish attempt on our part to be our own god. If only we took off our blinders, we would see that when we draw lines, they always seem to benefit us and hinder others. Our lines leverage our strengths, hide our weaknesses, and become more blurry the closer we get to sin. Soon, black and white start to look gray. If we make a habit of walking the line, we will eventually abuse God's grace and mercy as we recklessly cross back and forth.

God does not call us to see how close we can get to sin without sinning. He calls us to flee from even the appearance of evil (1 Thessalonians 5:22). This is what Joseph did when Potiphar's wife approached him. He didn't stick around to see how far he could go with her without actually sinning. He ran! If only we ran from temptations instead of entertaining them. In contrast, when David saw Bathsheba bathing on the rooftop, he didn't flee, he stayed. Perhaps he thought, "It's okay to look, as long as you don't touch." Or maybe he thought, "I am the King. I have served God well and I deserve to have a little fun. God will understand. He'll forgive." Regardless of what he thought, he stayed too long and the temptation to take what was not his overpowered him. This is a lesson through which we should all take heed. The longer you behold a temptation, the stronger it gets. That is why God calls us to flee from temptation. When we flee temptation, we abandon the pigsty and head towards the loving arms of our Father, who enables us to run and not grow weary (**Isaiah 40:31**). He wants us to win the race against our souls by running to Him.

16

Asleep

Then he returned to his disciples and found them sleeping.
"Simon," he said to Peter, "are you asleep?
Couldn't you keep watch for one hour?"
Mark 14:37 (NIV)

In April of 1999, I went to prom and had a great time dancing with friends. Afterwards, I went to the seniors' after party. As the night wore on, a couple of fights broke out, and my girlfriend, who was a junior, wanted to leave and go to the juniors' after party. It's important to note that back in the day, the junior class hated our senior class, although to be honest it was not without reason. Our class made their lives miserable with constant pranks, egg wars, brawls and any other awful thing we could think of doing. I knew I would not be a welcome guest at their party, but since my girlfriend wanted to go, and I am the living definition of chivalry (kidding), I took her.

As night became morning, some of the guys at the party, who had obviously had one too many wine coolers, tried to stir up a fight. Now I have never been one to back down from a fight, but I do recognize when I'm in a lose-lose situation. So I decided to leave before I became involved, and my girlfriend and I said our goodbyes. Then, I headed home.

As I was driving through town, I saw the sun rise over the horizon and a light fog roll across the frost-covered ground. That beautiful moment is the last thing I remember before being jolted by a blam that shook me awake. I had driven my car into the rear-end of a parked car. Both cars were totaled. Seconds later the police arrived, and knowing that prom was that night, they assumed I had been drinking, but I had not had a single drop of alcohol. I had simply fallen asleep at the wheel.

As I wondered how I could have possibly fallen asleep while driving, I retraced the journey in my mind. I realized I had probably driven a mile or more, weaving down the road, before getting off track, and miraculously driving between two trees, before jumping a curb, and hitting the only other car in a one mile radius.

Although driving drunk is an intentional choice and driving asleep is typically the result of not being mindful, both lead to a loss of control, safety, destiny and life. We fall asleep spiritually long before we die spiritually. Comfortable in our patterns of behavior, we allow ourselves to be lulled into a state of numbness toward our relationship with God. Many of us fall asleep and manage to go some distance before we see the impact of an autopilot lifestyle.

Like falling asleep, spiritual death does not happen immediately. It's a gradual process. First, our eyes become heavy with deception. Then, our hearts become hardened to God and His ways. Finally, we find ourselves living lives that have become tiresomely disobedient.

When God told Adam and Eve not to eat from the Tree of the Knowledge of Good and Evil or they would die, they must have believed Him, since they hadn't touched the fruit earlier. Had they been vigilant in obeying God and seeking him when presented with options that countered His instructions, they might not have fallen into sin. Somewhere along the way, they became casual about the things God said, which opened the door for doubt and disobedience.

Now the serpent was more crafty than any other beast of the field that the Lord God had made. He said to the woman, "Did God actually say, You shall not eat of any tree in the garden?" And the woman said to the serpent, "We may eat of the fruit of the trees in the garden, but God said, 'You shall not eat of the fruit of the tree that is in the midst of the garden, neither shall you touch it, lest you die.'" But the serpent said to the woman, "You will not surely die. For God knows that when you eat of it your eyes will be opened, and you will be like God, knowing good and evil." So when the woman saw that the tree was good for food, and that it was a delight to the eyes, and that the tree was to be desired to make one wise, she took of its fruit and ate, and she also gave some to her husband who was with her, and he ate. Then the eyes of both were opened, and they knew that they were naked. And they sewed fig leaves together and made themselves loincloths. **Genesis 3:1-7 (ESV)**

When Adam and Eve disobeyed God, they did not immediately die physically, but they did begin the process of dying. If death had come as soon as they disobeyed God's command, none of us would be here. Oftentimes the enemy uses delayed consequences as a strategy to lull us into the deception that God will not really judge our actions. Ironically, God's decision to delay consequences are actually the immediate manifestation of His grace and mercy toward us. Rather than giving us what we deserve, He gives us ample time to repent because He longs to forgive and restore us to a right relationship with Him.

The Lord is not slow to fulfill his promise as some count slowness, but is patient toward you, not wishing that any should perish, but that all should reach repentance. **2 Peter 3:9 (ESV)**

I believe it is a misunderstanding of the term "death" that sometimes leads us to dismiss God's warnings. Most people think of death as purely physical. To us, it is ceasing to breathe or exist. To gain a better understanding of what the word death means in the story of Adam and Eve, let's take a closer look at its origin and meaning. As is often the way with God, there are deep meanings hidden in plain sight in the simplest of things. The word used for "death" in Genesis comes from the ancient Hebrew pictograph for "chaos." According to the Holman Bible Dictionary, nouns that convey the Old Testament meaning of chaos include: emptiness; formless; waste; desolation; void; without light; a place of deep shadow, of utter gloom without order; forces of confusion; a wilderness unfit for habitation. Hebrew verbs describing chaos include: sinking into obscurity; becoming nothingness; falling prey to weakness. Holman goes on to state that the Hebrews personified chaos as "the principal opponent of God" and "a roaring sea," which is why the pictograph features a symbol for water. Holman states:

> "The chaos theme is implied, if not used, in the New Testament depicting God's victory in Christ. In the Gospels Christ confidently demonstrated mastery over the sea [chaos] (Mark 4:35-41 , Mark 6:45-52 ; John 6:16-21). In Revelation, when the ancient serpent, personified as the satanic dragon, rises out of the sea challenging His kingdom, Christ utterly defeats the adversary forever. So, beginning with Genesis 1:2, when God conquered the formless waste, and continuing through all the Scriptures, God's mighty power over chaos is shown repeatedly. Finally, the triumphal note is sounded in Revelation 21:1, "there was no more sea [chaos]." A new heaven and new earth are proof once again that chaos is conquered!"

1298) †ᴍ (מת *MT*) AC: **Die** CO: **Man** AB: **Mortality:** The pictograph ᴍ is a picture of water representing chaos, the † is a picture of two crossed sticks representing a mark or sign. Combined these mean "chaos mark". The length of time that something exists and ends. (eng: mute; moot - as a dead point; mortal - with an additional r and l; mate - of "check mate" meaning "king is dead")

A) †ᴍ (מת *MT*) AC: **?** CO: **Man** AB: **Mortality:** A length of time that comes to an end.

N^m) †ᴍ (מת *MT*) - Man: As mortal. KJV (22): man, few, friend, number, person, small - **Strongs:** H4962 (מֹת)

f^m) ᴊ†ᴍ (מתי *MTY*) - When: An unknown duration of time. KJV (3): when, long - **Strongs:** H4970 (מָתַי)

J) †Yᴍ (מות *MWT*) AC: **Die** CO: **?** AB: **Death:** The end of time for what has died.

The pictograph for chaos contains a symbol for water with a cross before it. How amazing is it that the cross was depicted as preceding chaos [the sea] before the Hebrew language was founded or crucifixion was invented? Jesus truly is the Alpha and the Omega and He sees the beginning from the end. I am grateful that His death on the cross, and subsequent resurrection, marks the ends of death and victory over chaos for us.[25]

Death has physical, spiritual, emotional and relational aspects, but for now, we will focus on spiritual death, taking a closer look at its three primary characteristics: despair, separation and denial.

Despair

The Random House Unabridged Dictionary defines despair as the complete loss or absence of hope. To be spiritually dead is to live without the hope Jesus brings to our hearts, minds and souls. People who are spiritually dead may appear to have life on the outside, but inside their souls are achingly empty and devoid of light. An example of this is seen in the many celebrities who commit suicide or overdose on drugs. Millions of people envy their lifestyles believing they have it all, but in reality their lives are in despair.

Please do not misunderstand me, I am not saying that if you struggle with depression that you are spiritually dead. What I am saying is that depression is a form of despair, and sometimes it is a symptom of the onset of spiritual death. Other times depression is a byproduct of mental illness, unresolved stress or a chemical imbalance. If you suffer from depression, please contact a good Christian counselor who can help you process your pain and overcome depression.

Separation

Webster's dictionary defines chaos as a chasm or abyss. In other words death is a form of separation defined by distance. It is the space created between people by sin. We see the separation inherent in death in the story Jesus tells of Lazarus and the Rich Man.

"There was a rich man who was dressed in purple and fine linen and lived in luxury every day. At his gate laid a beggar named Lazarus, covered with sores and longing to eat what fell from the rich man's table. Even the dogs came and licked his sores.

The time came when the beggar died and the angels carried him to Abraham's side. The rich man also died and was buried. In Hades, where he was in torment, he looked up and saw Abraham far away, with Lazarus by his side. So he called to him, 'Father Abraham, have pity on me and send Lazarus to dip the tip of his finger in water and cool my tongue, because I am in agony in this fire.'

> "But Abraham replied, 'Son, remember that in your lifetime you received your good things, while Lazarus received bad things, but now he is comforted here and you are in agony. And besides all this, between us and you a great chasm has been set in place, so that those who want to go from here to you cannot, nor can anyone cross over from there to us.'
>
> "He answered, 'Then I beg you, father, send Lazarus to my family, for I have five brothers. Let him warn them, so that they will not also come to this place of torment.'
>
> "Abraham replied, 'They have Moses and the Prophets; let them listen to them.'
>
> "'No, father Abraham,' he said, 'but if someone from the dead goes to them, they will repent.'
>
> "He said to him, 'If they do not listen to Moses and the Prophets, they will not be convinced even if someone rises from the dead.'" **Luke 16:19-31 (NIV)**

Death creates a chasm between the living and the dead. Sin is always divisive. It separates us from God and leads to death. Moreover, it is completely possible to be physically alive and spiritually dead at the same time. Paul talks about this paradox in **Ephesians 2:4-5 (NIV)**: But because of his great love for us, God, who is rich in mercy, made us alive with Christ even when we were dead in transgressions—it is by grace you have been saved.

If you have not been made alive by inviting Christ to be the Lord of your life, then you are spiritually dead.

It is important to note that the distance death brings between us and God is not a byproduct of God's anger or wrath. It is created by our disobedience. **God does not move away from us. His love is constant. He moves towards us. We are the ones who move away from Him.** We choose, through disobedience, to go in the opposite direction of His will, love and Kingdom.

Let's look at the story of Adam and Eve again.

> Then the man and his wife heard the sound of the Lord God as he was walking in the garden in the cool of the day, and they hid from the Lord God among the trees of the garden. But the Lord God called to the man, "Where are you?"
>
> He answered, "I heard you in the garden, and I was afraid because I was naked; so I hid."
>
> And he said, "Who told you that you were naked? Have you eaten from the tree that I commanded you not to eat from?"
>
> The man said, "The woman you put here with me—she gave me some fruit from the tree, and I ate it."
>
> Then the Lord God said to the woman, "What is this you have done?"
>
> The woman said, "The serpent deceived me, and I ate."
> **Genesis 3:8-13 (NIV)**

When Adam and Eve disobeyed God, who moved? They did. Their eyes were opened to their guilt and shame, which led them away from God, not toward Him. That's how sin creates distance.

Where was God after Adam and Eve sinned? He was looking for them. Even in our disobedience, God pursues us. When we fall, He wants to pick us up. God's love for us is constant regardless of our response to Him.

> But God showed his great love for us by sending Christ
> to die for us while we were still sinners.
> **Romans 5:8 (ESV)**

God's first question to Adam and Eve was not, "What did you do?" or "What were you thinking?" He did not angrily declare, "I can't leave you two alone for one minute without you messing everything up!"
No, His first question was, "Where are you?" God wanted to close the distance between them.

God's love for you is unrelenting and faithful. No one will ever love you as much as He does — not your spouse, parents, children, friends or pets. You can always count on Him. His love does not change. It is constant. No other love can compare.

We've all been to weddings and church services and heard the passage from Corinthians that offers God's definition of love. It is simultaneously inspiring and convicting as we realize how far short we fall of His standard. The good news is God not only sets the standard, He fulfills it. As you read the passage below, I want you to see God in the role as the lover and yourself as His beloved.

> Love is patient and kind; love does not envy or
> boast; it is not arrogant or rude. It does not insist on
> its own way; it is not irritable or resentful; it does not
> rejoice at wrongdoing, but rejoices with the truth. Love
> bears all things, believes all things, hopes all things,
> endures all things. Love never ends.
> **1 Corinthians 13:4-8 (ESV)**

Corinthians describes in perfect detail how God loves us and what that looks and feels like. When we feel distant from God, it is our love that is inconsistent, not God's.

Imagine a 10-foot-wide street with God on one side and you on the other. When you get saved, you join God on His side, where you are in communion with Him. The relationship is intimate, trusting and free of shame. You are satisfied in Jesus. One day, you choose to sin. Perhaps you watch something inappropriate or get drunk at the company Christmas party. The shame and guilt from your sin causes you to take a step away from God. Your relationship which was once a "10" is now a nine. As your shame continues to eat at you, you put it out of your mind by avoiding spending time with God. You no longer read your Bible or pray. This creates even more distance between you and God, and the relationship declines to a six. As you continue to step out on God, you unwittingly move into the enemy's territory, and he begins to fill your head and heart with questions and doubts about God. You recognize that you are not as close to God as you used to be, and choose to believe the lie that God must be mad at you and has forsaken you because of your sin. The distance between you and God grows so much that others can see it. You feel alone and scared, and you believe that God is against you. At this point, you are running from anything that has to do with God, His Word or His church. There is a great distance between you and God that is tangible. This is the death God was referring to when He commanded Adam and Eve not to eat forbidden fruit.

When we feel distant, we usually blame God, but we're the ones who left. Like the parable of the prodigal son (Luke 15: 11-32), we took off on our own for a distant land. Meanwhile, God does not turn His back on us. No, He waits by the road, His eyes searching for any sign of our return. His love for us never wavers. Like His character, it is the same yesterday, today and tomorrow.

The amazing beauty of God's love is this — although It may take a long time and countless wrong steps to create distance between you and

God, it only takes one step to restore your relationship with Him, and that step is repentance. Repentance is acknowledging our disobedience and turning back to God. When we repent, shame and guilt lose their power. We are instantly restored to a close and intimate relationship with God.

Denial

Finally, death is characterized by denial. When someone we love physically dies, we experience the pain of being denied access to them. If, when we physically die, we are also spiritually dead, we experience the neverending pain, hopelessness, torment and chaos of being separated from God forever.

In our current culture, many false Christians preach that because God loves us, we can live however we want. Their highest priority is to please people, not God. Their messages center around teaching people how to get everything they want in life, and everything God has for them. They do not teach people about sacrificial love, or what it means to love God enough to pick up your cross, become like Him in His sufferings, and follow Him wherever He leads. Truths like those aren't crowd-pleasers.

> For a time is coming when people will no longer listen
> to sound and wholesome teaching. They will follow
> their own desires and will look for teachers who will tell
> them whatever their itching ears want to hear.
> **2 Timothy 4:3 (ESV)**

One of the saddest, most tragic, and sobering truths you will ever hear is this: Hell is real and Jesus says there will be MANY people that spend eternity there.

Not everyone who says to me, Lord, Lord, will enter the kingdom of heaven, but the one who does the will of my Father who is in heaven. On that day many will say to me, Lord, Lord, did we not prophesy in your name, and cast out demons in your name, and do many mighty works in your name? And then will I declare to them, I never knew you; depart from me, you workers of lawlessness.

Matthew 7:21-23 (ESV)

And I saw the dead, great and small, standing before the throne, and books were opened. Then another book was opened, which is the book of life. And the dead were judged by what was written in the books, according to what they had done. And the sea gave up the dead who were in it, Death and Hades gave up the dead who were in them, and they were judged, each one of them, according to what they had done. Then Death and Hades were thrown into the lake of fire. This is the second death, the lake of fire. And if anyone's name was not found written in the book of life, he was thrown into the lake of fire.

Revelation 20:12-15 (ESV)

There will be two groups of people at the end of time: those who are welcomed into God's Kingdom and those who are denied access. The determining factor of who is welcomed and who is denied is based on the Lamb's Book of Life. The prerequisite for whether or not your name is in the Lamb's Book of Life is are you in Christ or out of Christ. It is a simple question with great ramifications. If you are outside of Jesus, then God is going to judge you based on your works. If you are inside of Jesus, then God is going to judge you based on Jesus's works.

For you have died, and your life is hidden with Christ in God. When Christ who is your life appears, then you also will appear with him in glory.
Colossians 3:3-4 (ESV)

What shall we say then? Are we to continue in sin that grace may abound? By no means! How can we who died to sin still live in it? Do you not know that all of us who have been baptized into Christ Jesus were baptized into his death? We were buried therefore with him by baptism into death, in order that, just as Christ was raised from the dead by the glory of the Father, we too might walk in newness of life. For if we have been united with him in a death like his, we shall certainly be united with him in a resurrection like his. We know that our old self was crucified with him in order that the body of sin might be brought to nothing, so that we would no longer be enslaved to sin. For one who has died has been set free from sin. Now if we have died with Christ, we believe that we will also live with him. We know that Christ, being raised from the dead, will never die again; death no longer has dominion over him. For the death he died he died to sin, once for all, but the life he lives he lives to God. So you also must consider yourselves dead to sin and alive to God in Christ Jesus.
Romans 6:2-11 (ESV)

If you are in Christ you are in the Lamb's Book of Life. If you are not in Christ, you are denied access to Heaven. If you think this is too harsh, then you don't understand God's holiness and justice. God is a god of justice whether we like it or not.

You make God tired with all your talk.
"How do we tire him out?" you ask.
By saying, "God loves sinners and sin alike.
God loves all." And also by saying,
"Judgment? God's too nice to judge."
Malachi 2:17 (MSG)

When we fall asleep spiritually and end up dying spiritually, we miss out on the life God has for us and the victory He has promised us. Sleeping troops are easy targets. Awake soldiers stay alert so they may defeat the enemy's tactics.

1. Is your spiritual life awake or asleep?
2. Are you alert and actively pursuing
   God's purposes?
3. What can you do today to awaken your soul?

17

Destiny

Blessed is the man who remains steadfast under trial, for when he has stood the test he will receive the crown of life, which God has promised to those who love him.

James 1:12 (ESV)

James Harrison, a linebacker for the New England Patriots, is known as a tough football player who has no mercy on his opponents. Three years ago, he got more attention for his parenting strategy than his football skills. His children had received trophies, not for winning a championship or coming in second or third, but for simply participating. James Harrison was not happy about this and went to Instagram to let the world know.

"I came home to find out that my boys received two trophies for nothing, participation trophies! While I am very proud of my boys for everything they do and will encourage them till the day I die, these trophies will be given back until they EARN a real trophy. I'm not sorry for believing that everything in life should be earned, and I'm not about to raise two boys to be men by making them believe that they are entitled to something just because they tried their best...cause sometimes your best is not enough, and that should drive you to want to do better...not cry and whine until somebody gives you something to shut you up and keep you happy."[26]

James Harrison did not want his kids to falsely believe that everyone wins. He wanted to teach them that they have to accomplish something in order to win. I believe the mentality of participation trophies has infiltrated our churches in that we believe we can just say we are Christians and win. This is simply not true.

When we say yes to Jesus, we begin our race, and it is a marathon, not a sprint. A sprint tests the body, but a marathon tests the heart. The race we run will not go to the fastest, but to the one who endures all of the obstacles, trials and temptations along the way. To win, you must have discipline, perseverance and a willingness to push through pain and suffering. There may be times when you become weary and feel like quitting, but the prize is greater than your suffering. James (the disciple, not the linebacker), tells us the trophy that we are after is the Crown of Life. And Paul warns us that not everyone will receive this prize.

> Do you not know that in a race all the runners run, but only one gets the prize? Run in such a way as to get the prize. Everyone who competes in the games goes into strict training. They do it to get a crown that will not last, but we do it to get a crown that will last forever. Therefore I do not run like someone running aimlessly; I do not fight like a boxer beating the air. No, I strike a blow to my body and make it my slave so that after I have preached to others, I myself will not be disqualified for the prize.
> **1 Corinthians 9:24-27 (NIV)**

Your are in a race for your life. Your pain, suffering, patience, diligence and obedience are not in vain. There is a prize awaiting you at the finish line, when you take your last breath on earth and your first breath in heaven. It is a crown given to you by God in recognition that you have kept the faith and are truly a son or daughter of the King of Kings.

Don't Give Up

Make the decision today that you will not quit your race until you reach God's finish line. Don't quit on your marriage, your ministry, your children, or your walk with Jesus. Don't get distracted by how the world is running; they are on a broad path to destruction. The world loves speed, not endurance. Your enemy cannot stop you from running, but he will tempt you to believe lies such as:

Your race is in vain.

This pain is not worth it.

You can't go any further.

You're never going to make it.

God understands how hard it is and He'll forgive you if you quit.

Commit Not to Quit

To win the race of faith, you must commit not to quit — no matter what. Keep trusting God and His promises. Set your mind on things above and seek Him first. Be steadfast. The Greek word for steadfast means to remain. We are called to remain in Jesus, in the faith, and on the path God has set before us. If the enemy puts a mountain in your way, don't leave your path to go around it, tell it to move.

> "Truly, I say to you, whoever says to this mountain, 'Be taken up and thrown into the sea,' and does not doubt in his heart, but believes that what he says will come to pass, it will be done for him. Therefore I tell you, whatever you ask in prayer, believe that you have received it, and it will be yours." **Mark 11:23-24 (ESV)**

When you partner with God to move mountains, you almost always are clearing a path for others to follow in their pursuit of God. Perhaps your children and grandchildren, or your church, city or neighbors will accomplish great things for the Kingdom of God because your faithfulness and perseverance helped pave a path through their wilderness. As believers, we are part of a racing team and our efforts impact the lives of those around us and those who will come behind us.

Greg Lemond has one of the greatest comeback stories in sports. He was a professional cyclist who won his first Tour de France in 1986. He had planned to defend his Tour de France title in 1987, but fractured his wrist and took time to recover. During this time, he went on a turkey hunting trip with his uncle and brother-in-law and was accidentally shot. Sixty pellets were embedded in his back and right side and he was life-flighted to a hospital for emergency surgery. Later, his surgeon said Lemond was 20 minutes away from bleeding to death when he arrived at the hospital. Although the surgery was considered a success, only 25 of the pellets were removed. The remaining 35 were inoperable.

Eventually Lemond recovered from surgery and wanted to get back into professional cycling. He entered the 1989 Tour de France with a goal of finishing in the top 20. Lemond used the first week of the race's stages to recondition himself to the difficult terrain. During the final stages, he cycled at a pace that many thought was unachievable. He took the lead and began pushing harder. His body, with its 35 shotgun pellets ached with fatigue, but he kept telling himself, "Don't quit. Keep going. If you don't quit now, you will become a champion!" Lemond won the 1989 Tour de France by the slimmest margin ever, eight seconds, but he also set a record for the fastest pace in the final stage. Two years earlier he almost died. Now, he stood on the podium, a champion.

If you don't quit, you will be a champion, too. Yes, the race is difficult and it feels like everything is against you. Your body aches and your heart hurts, but you can and must keep going. James tells us that all of the pain we endure will be worth it when we finish. Paul echoes his words in his letter to the Romans.

> For I consider that the sufferings of this present time are not worth comparing with the glory that is to be revealed to us. Romans 8:18 (ESV)

Steadfastness, endurance, and perseverance are not natural abilities. They are developed as we suffer various trials. One of the things I think is incredible about God is that when he allows us to face trials, He is showing us that He believes in us. He knows what He has placed inside us and that through His Son we have the power to endure and to overcome any obstacle. Oftentimes He allows us to go through difficulties so that we can discover who He is and who we are in Him.

No temptation has overtaken you that is not common to man. God is faithful, and he will not let you be tempted beyond your ability, but with the temptation he will also provide the way of escape, that you may be able to endure it. **1 Corinthians 10:13 (ESV)**

I believe there are four keys to endurance that will help you finish your race and reach your destiny:

1. Know why you are running.
2. Remember you aren't alone.
3. Run for the finish line.
4. Keep your eyes on the prize.

Why Are You Running?

The reason you said yes to the gospel of Jesus in your heart and mind is because God called you to Himself. You realized your need for His salvation and were overwhelmed by His unconditional love. You knew He chose you and that He wants you with Him at the finish line of your life. You understood the race was real, the consequences were eternal, and that Jesus had not only prepared the way, but would be with you at every step. Paul reminded the church at Thessalonica why they were running in order to encourage them to keep going.

> Now may the God of peace himself sanctify you completely, and may your whole spirit and soul and body be kept blameless at the coming of our Lord Jesus Christ. He who calls you is faithful; he will surely do it.
> **1 Thessalonians 5:23-24 (ESV)**

> God called you and He is faithful to the end. And I am certain that God, who began the good work within you, will continue his work until it is finally finished on the day when Christ Jesus returns.
> **Philippians 1:6 (NLT)**

You Are Not Alone

> Therefore, since we are surrounded by such a great cloud of witnesses, let us throw off every encumbrance and the sin that so easily entangles, and let us run with endurance the race set out for us."
> **Hebrews 12:1 (NIV)**

We do not run our race in isolation. There are people at all points of the way who are watching us run. Some are fellow believers looking for insight and encouragement. Some are interested in where we are going. Some want to know why we choose to run. And some are antagonists who don't want us to win because they are not willing to run their own race. The great leader Nehemiah faced bystanders who wanted to see him fail. Sanballat and Tobiah were witnesses of Nehemiah's walk with God and they wanted to see him fail and quit.

> When Sanballat heard that we were rebuilding the wall,
> he became angry and was greatly incensed. He ridi-
> culed the Jews, and in the presence of his associates and
> the army of Samaria, he said, "What are those feeble
> Jews doing? Will they restore their wall? Will they offer
> sacrifices? Will they finish in a day? Can they bring the
> stones back to life from those heaps of rubble—burned
> as they are?" Tobiah the Ammonite, who was at his side,
> said, "What they are building—even a fox climbing up
> on it would break down their wall of stones!"
> **Nehemiah 4:1-3 (NIV)**

As you run, the enemy will seek to antagonize, discourage and oppose your efforts, but he is not a match for the greatest witness to your race, your friend, coach and trusted ally, God. As Paul states in Romans 8:31 (ESV), "...If God is for us, who can be against us?" God also gives you friends, family and fellow believers to help you go the distance. Knowing others are pulling for you should inspire you to run faster and farther, and be even more determined to overcome all obstacles. When Sanballat began opposing Nehemiah, Nehemiah encouraged himself and others who were witnesses to his life.

And I looked and arose and said to the nobles and to the

officials and to the rest of the people, Do not be afraid of
them. Remember the Lord, who is great and awesome,
and fight for your brothers, your sons,
your daughters, your wives, and your homes.
Nehemiah 4:14 (ESV)

Run for the Finish Line

When I was in the Air Force, I was stationed in Pensacola, Florida. Physical training tests were conducted at midnight due to the heat and humidity. Each night, we ran two miles on an inactive runway at an old airfield. In order to mark the one mile mark, one of our drill sergeants would drive a van a mile down the runway and turn the headlights on. We would run towards two headlights in the dark, but it often seemed liked the more we ran, the farther the headlights got. I'm still not convinced our drill sergeant didn't put the van in reverse and move away from us as we ran. I do recall always feeling a tremendous surge of relief whenever I reached the van because the way back was the home stretch.

You have to focus on running for the finish line if you want to run your race well. Coaches, from athletic to life and everything in between, know that setting a goal with a destination in mind is one of the first and most critical steps a person must take in order to achieve anything. A second step that is essential to achieving goals is taking action. God designed us to overcome obstacles and experience victory. One of the ways He trains us to be overcomers is by building our faith and capabilities through a series of smaller victories. No one wakes up an Olympic champion. Olympians must first undergo a lifetime of training, overcoming obstacles and winning minor victories that culminate in the ultimate victory. Our walk with God is similar. Each obstacle and victory we experience is a mile marker God uses to remind us of how far we've come as He guides us toward a successful finish.

Every person in this world was created to do a series of good things and we can see the manifestations of this truth in stories throughout the Bible. Nehemiah's work was to restore the walls of Jerusalem. Esther's work was to help save the people of Israel. Jesus' work of salvation and redemption for all was fulfilled on the cross. God has good works for you to do, too.

> For we are God's masterpiece. He has created us anew in Christ Jesus, so we can do the good things he planned for us long ago.
> **Ephesians 2:10 (NLT)**
>
> And whatever you do or say, do it as a representative of the Lord Jesus, giving thanks throughhim to God the Father.
> **Colossians 3:17 (NLT)**

Beyond completing good works, God wants you to finish your race of faith, where He will be waiting to embrace you, love you, and bless you with the joy of His eternal presence. If there is breath in your body, God is calling you to run, regardless of your age or abilities. Your race to finish life with a thriving faith is not a part-time gig you can train for whenever you feel motivated. It is a matter of life and death, with a destination of heaven or hell. There will be winners and losers. Run for your life. Race to win.

Keep Your Eye on the Prize

There is a crown of life for those whose faith endures to the end. Some translators refer to this crown as "life and more life," meaning that God will cause you to experience more life than you ever dreamed possible. This is the abundant life Jesus promised that brings everlasting peace, overflowing joy and eternal hope.

> "The thief comes only to steal and kill and destroy. I came that they may have life and have it abundantly."
> John 10:10 (ESV)

The Bible teaches that there are five crowns that Jesus gives away [27]: a crown of life, a crown of victory, a crown of glory, a crown of righteousness, and a crown of honor. These crowns are incorruptible and imperishable eternal rewards.

The Crown of Life

James and John tell us the crown of life is given to those who persevere under trials and are faithful even to the point of death.

> Blessed is the man who remains steadfast under trial,
> for when he has stood the test he will receive the **crown
> of life**, which God has promised to those who love him.
> **James 1:12 (ESV)**

> Do not fear what you are about to suffer. Behold,
> the devil is about to throw some of you into prison,
> that you may be tested, and for ten days you
> will have tribulation. Be faithful unto death,
> and I will give you the **crown of life**.
> **Revelation 2:10 (ESV)**

The Incorruptible Crown aka The Imperishable Crown

Paul tells us that the imperishable crown is given to those who have self-restraint and self-discipline.

> And everyone who competes for the prize is temperate in all things. Now they do it to obtain a perishable crown, but we for an **imperishable crown.**
> **1 Corinthians 9:25 (ESV)**

Crown of Righteousness

Paul states that a crown of righteousness is given to those who love and anticipate Jesus' return.

> Finally, there is laid up for me the **crown of righteousness,** which the Lord, the righteous Judge, will give to me on that Day, and not to me only but also to all who have loved His appearing.
> **2 Timothy 4:8 (NKJV)**

Crown of Glory

Peter says that leaders who share in Christ's sufferings and shepherd God's people with care and a willing heart will receive a crown of glory.

> Be shepherds of God's flock that is under your care, watching over them—not because you must, but because you are willing, as God wants you to be; not

pursuing dishonest gain, but eager to serve; not lording
it over those entrusted to you, but being examples to the
flock. And when the Chief Shepherd appears, you will
receive the **crown of glory** that will never fade away.
1 Peter 5:2-4 (NIV)

Crown of Rejoicing

Paul says that the crown of rejoicing is given to those who share the
good news and who remain steadfast in their faith in Jesus.

For what is our hope or joy or **crown of rejoicing**
before our Lord Jesus at his coming? Is it not you
For you are our glory and joy.
1 Thessalonians 2:19-20 (ESV)

Therefore, my brothers, whom I love and long
for, my joy and crown, stand firm thus in the
Lord, my beloved. **Philippians 4:1 (ESV)**

The King of Kings has a crown for you.
Run toward Him with all you've got for all of your life.
He has set a finish line before you and has given you all
you need to finish well. Make it your mission in life to
be able to say, as Paul did, "I have fought the good
fight, I have finished the race, I have kept the faith."
(2 Timothy 4:7, ESV)

Then you will hear Jesus say,
"Well done, good and faithful servant."
Matthew 25:21 (ESV)

18

Crown

"You will also be a crown of beauty in the hand of the LORD, And a royal diadem in the hand of your God."
Isaiah 62:3 (NAS)

Imagine you are sitting in a large stadium surrounded by friends, family and thousands upon thousands of happy people. There is a palpable undercurrent of joy fueling the atmosphere. The crowd goes quiet and you hear an MC say:

Ladies and Gentlemen,
It is my honor to introduce a Man who needs no introduction. Although his credits are too long to list, we'll start by saying He has done the impossible time after time. He hails from a manger in Bethlehem by way of Heaven. His mother is known as the most blessed among women. His Father is the Author of the number one best-selling book of all time. He holds the record for the world's greatest fish catch, and once fed five thousand people with two fish and five loaves of bread. He can walk on water and turn water into wine. He is the King of all kings, the Ruler of the universe, the Alpha and the Omega, the Bright and Morning Star, the Rose of Sharon, and your Prince of Peace.

Get to your feet; put your hands together; and show your love for the second coming of the one and only... Our Lord...Our Savior...Our Redeemer...Our King...Jesus Christ.

The crowd erupts in cheers that sound like thunder rolling, and it is the most beautiful sound you have ever heard. You look upon Jesus and shout praises to Him at the top of your lungs. The crowd is united in praise and its power shakes the stadium like a mighty earthquake.

King Jesus enters and sits on a beautiful, majestic throne. Your eyes are transfixed by His beauty. His eyes glow with a fiery love and His powerful and authoritative, yet loving and encouraging voice welcomes everyone to the celebration.

Jesus talks about how He has waited for this glorious day of celebration. He reflects upon how His now defeated enemy tried to stop this day from happening but failed because God's plans are always greater. He talks about how God's plan for His people is fulfilled in this very moment. He talks about His plan to bless His people with His love and presence, and His desire to establish a Kingdom on earth just like there is in Heaven. He then describes the plan to choose for Himself a people, how He gave them a Law that showed them His standard of holiness and pointed them to His perfect sacrifice. He tells how He left heaven, gave up His glory and divine benefits to come to earth to demonstrate the love and ways of His Father.

The crowd erupts in thunderous praise and you marvel at the goodness of God. You are thankful and amazed at how Jesus worked His plan in your life over and over again. And now, you have crossed the finish line. The conflict between God's plan for your life and the enemy's plan to disrupt it is over, and God has given you a great victory.

After the crowd quiets down, a man steps up to the podium and opens an extremely large book. Jesus stands and as the man reads the names, He shares His love and affirmation for each person, recalling personal stories of their trials, sufferings, persecution, losses and victories. In a moment of clarity, you see that just like the people in the Bible, everyone's personal story has a common thread of God's unwavering love. His invisible hand in all our lives is mesmerizingly clear. In every high and low, Jesus is there, doing what love does — being patient and kind, selflessly honoring others, clearing our record of wrongs and rejoicing with us in truth. He has and will always protect us, be worthy of our trust, fulfill our hopes, and remain when all else is gone. He truly is God with us and His love never fails.

As you ponder His goodness in your heart, a flash of light catches your eyes. The Lord has in his hand one of the most exquisite and beautiful things you have ever seen, a royal crown encrusted with a spectrum of perfect jewels in every color known to man, as well as quite a few colors you have never seen before.
He places the crown on the person standing before him. It is an awesome scene to behold and the crowd erupts with praise for God once again.

You are lost in praise, wondering at the goodness and glory of Jesus when you hear your own name called. It is a joy that is almost too wonderful to bear. You make your way to Him, and upon seeing Him face-to-face, His love overwhelms you and you fall at his feet in total worship. He gently raises you up and you notice the nail-scars on his hands, and in his eyes you see an ocean's depth of love and compassion. He Steps towards you and wraps His arms around you and as you sink into His embrace everything in your past, all the pain, suffering, shame, and fear, are gone, never to return again.

The embrace ends and Jesus begins telling your story. He recalls the day you met, and as He speaks you marvel at the great love that saw you when you were broken, sinful, disobedient, addicted, hopeless, sick, and ashamed, and yet, chose you, loved you, pursued and wanted you. His love was not deterred by your family dysfunction, the pain you experienced or the pain you caused. He loved you through times of sickness, disease, and personal tragedy. His love remained when you were plagued by fears. He was there when everyone else abandoned you. He did not forsake you when you doubted His existence. He remained steadfast. When the enemy tried to get you to quit your race and disrupt God's plan for your life, He gave you strength. When your loved ones died and you felt consumed by grief, he comforted you because He understands pain, loss and grief like no one else. He heard every one of your prayers and collected every tear you shed. Jesus shares how proud He is of you that you overcame temptations and endured difficult seasons. You persevered in suffering when others gave up or quit, but not you.

Finally, He tells the crowd you are a champion of the faith. You have run your race and finished well.

He then turns to you and says, "Well done my good and faithful servant. Welcome home to eternal peace and rest." The crowd cheers wildly and you look at your heavenly family for a moment before returning your attention to Jesus. You gasp as you see He is holding a gloriously beautiful crown, dripping with an array of sparkling jewels. Jesus holds the crown up so that everyone can see your achievement in Him and His reward for you for finishing your race.

Then He places the crown on your head and you are instantly filled with an overflow of peace, gratitude, joy, and hope. It is at this moment that you realize every trial and storm, all the suffering and pain were worth it.

Your joy will never end. You have inherited the abundant life Jesus promised. Your crown will never fade or perish. This is your new reality, and it is just the beginning.

> And I heard a loud voice from the throne saying, "Look! God's dwelling place is now among the people, and he will dwell with them. They will be his people, and God himself will be with them and be their God. 'He will wipe every tear from their eyes. There will be no more death or mourning or crying or pain, for the old order of things

has passed away." He who was seated on the throne said, "I am making everything new!" Then he said, "Write this down, for these words are trustworthy and true." He said to me: "It is done. I am the Alpha and the Omega, the Beginning and the End. To the thirsty I will give water without cost from the spring of the water of life. Those who are victorious will inherit all this, and I will be their God and they will be my children." **Revelation 21:3-7 (NIV)**

Epilogue

For this light momentary affliction is preparing for us an eternal weight of glory beyond all comparison, as we look not to the things that are seen but to the things that are unseen. For the things that are seen are transient, but the things that are unseen are eternal. **2 Corinthians 4:17-18 (ESV)**

I want to encourage you that no matter what you are suffering, or how great your pain, if you hold onto Jesus and resolve to endure, it will all be worth it. No matter how strong the temptations are that befall you or how great the obstacles appear in front of you, if you persevere in your faith in Him, it will all be worth it. Wherever you are in your race, do not let the enemy's tactics entice you to quit. Jesus is worth giving your all, and He has a crown waiting for you at the finish line.

Afterword

Most of the time when I am asked to write a comment, a forward or an insightful thought to recommend a book I deal with the subject, content or personal value to the reader. As I gave consideration to this book I really wanted the people to know the author, Bobby Gourley. I have known Bobby for a number of years. I have known him as parishioner, staff pastor, campus pastor and now Lead Pastor. I have observed his life both with his wife, children and other relationships. He is the real deal when it comes to faith and insightful thinking. I visit with him often, glean from him on a regular basis and enjoy being his friend. If the foundation for a good message is a godly man this book is ready to change the landscape of the city you live in…it will lift you to a place of higher thinking, more fruitful living and being a better person.

– MAURY DAVIS
MAURY DAVIS MINISTRIES

Notes

Chapter 1

1. Tony Evans, *Victory In Spiritual Warfare* Eugene: Harvest House Publishers, 2011.

Chapter 2

2. "Invent | Definition Of Invent In English By Oxford Dictionaries", Oxford Dictionaries | English, Last modified 2019, https://en.oxforddictionaries.com/definition/invent.

Chapter 3

3. "Strong's #622 - Ἀπόλλυμι - Old & New Testament Greek Lexicon", Studylight.Org, Last modified 2019, https://www.studylight.org/lexicons/greek/622.html.

Chapter 4

4. Wilson, Μιχαήλ. ""We Can Only Hope For What We Desire." ~~C. S. Lewis". Jesus Quotes And God Thoughts, Last modified 2019. https://quotesthoughtsrandom.wordpress.com/2016/09/03/we-can-only-hope-for-what-we-desire-c-s-lewis/.

5 Tony Evans, Tony Evans' Book Of Illustrations Chicago, IL: Moody Publishers, 2009.

Chapter 5

6 Andrews, Andy, and Andy Andrews. Mastering The Seven Decisions That Determine Personal Success. Petaling Jaya, Selangor: Advantage Quest Pub., 2009.

7 Russell D Moore, Tempted And Tried Wheaton, IL: Crossway, 2011.

8 John Eldredge, The Journey Of Desire Nashville: Thomas Nelson Publishers, 2000.

Chapter 6

9. Steven Reiss, Who Am I? New York, NY: Berkeley Books280, 2002.

Chapter 7

10 John Piper, "The War Within: Flesh Versus Spirit", Desiring God, Last modified 2019, https://www.desiringgod.org/messages/the-war-within-flesh-versus-spirit.

Chapter 9

11 John Eldredge, The Journey Of Desire Nashville: Thomas Nelson Publishers, 2000.

12 "What Does It Mean To Be Filled With The Spirit?", Keepbelieving.Com, Last modified 2019, https://www.keepbelieving.com/sermon/what-does-it-mean-to-be-filled-with-the-spirit/.

Chapter 10

13 Society, National. "Fall Of Troy". National Geographic Society, Last modified 2019. https://www.nationalgeographic.org/thisday/apr24/fall-troy/.

14 Heyward-Mills, Dag. Loyalty And Disloyalty. Great Britain: Sunpenny Publishing Group, 2013.

Chapter 11

15 "Our Daily Bread Experience". Odb.Org, Last modified 2019. https://odb.org/2010/01/26/delayed-consequences/.

Chapter 12

16 "Judge Calls For Prison Time In Texting And Driving Manslaughter Case", AL.Com, Last modified 2019, https://www.al.com/news/mobile/index.ssf/2016/04/judge_calls_for_prison_time_in.html.

17 Sermon Illustrations. Accessed February 15, 2019. http://www.sermonillustrations.com/a-z/c/counterfeit.htm.

18 "Inattentional Blindness." Wikipedia. February 12, 2019. Accessed February 15, 2019. https://en.wikipedia.org/wiki/Inattentional_blindness.

Chapter 13

19 Sermon Illustrations. Accessed February 15, 2019. http://www.sermonillustrations.com/a-z/c/counterfeit.htm.

20 Tim Challies. "Counterfeit Detection (Part 1)." Tim Challies. November 25, 2016. Accessed February 15, 2019. https://www.challies.com/articles/counterfeit-detection-part-1/.

21 Stetzer, Ed. "New Research: Less Than 20% of Churchgoers Read the Bible Daily." Christian History | Learn the History of Christianity & the Church. Accessed

February 15, 2019. https://www.christianitytoday.com/edstetzer/2012/september/
new-research-less-than-20-of-churchgoers-read-bible-daily.html.

Chapter 14
22 Giannini, Darleen, Reader's Digest, February, 1995, p. 59

Chapter 15
23 Vaden, Rory. Take the Stairs: 7 Steps to Achieving True Success. New York: Peri-
gee/Penguin, 2013.

24 "Sin Is Cosmic Treason." Ligonier Ministries. Accessed February 15, 2019. https://
www.ligonier.org/blog/sin-cosmic-treason/.

Chapter 16
25 Pictograph citation: Strong's #4191 - מות - Old Testament Hebrew Lexicon."
StudyLight.org. Accessed March 07, 2019. https://www.studylight.org/lexicons/
hebrew/4191.html.

Chapter 17
26 Boren, Cindy. "James Harrison Thinks Kids' Participation Trophies Are Worthless,
Sets off Debate." The Washington Post. August 16, 2015. Accessed February 15,
2019. https://www.washingtonpost.com/news/early-lead/wp/2015/08/16/james-
harrison-wont-let-his-kids-get-participation-trophies/?noredirect=on&utm_
term=.2161c239ab75.

27 "5 Types of Crowns in Heaven." Christian Truth Center. October 20, 2015.
Accessed February 15, 2019. http://www.christiantruthcenter.com/5-types-of-crowns-
in-heaven/.

Resources

Fasting by Jentezen Franklin

7 Basic Steps to Successful Fasting and Prayer by Dr. Bill Bright
(https://www.cru.org/us/en/train-and-grow/spiritual-growth/fasting/7-steps-to-fast-
ing.html)

Atomic Power with God through Prayer & Fasting by Franklin Hall

Made in the USA
Middletown, DE
21 March 2019